"A book of luminous verse, at once prayer templative's companion. Its words offer a doorway into the realm of holy ground, opening up the possibility of intimacy with the Sacred by way of immersion in selected psalms."

—**Julie McGonegal,** author of *Imagining Justice: The Politics of Postcolonial Forgiveness and Reconciliation*

"*Random and Nebulous—Nuancing the Psalms* is a wonderful addition to your devotional collection. Janis has gathered some of the best-loved psalms and breathed new life into them. . . . Enjoy each stanza, caring for yourself—your soul—as you bathe in the *Holy Lovelight*, taking time to ponder and to pray as you go. Selah."

—**Michelle O'Rourke**, author of *Befriending Death: Henri Nouwen and a Spirituality of Dying*

"If you have ever read a psalm, you need this book. Janis has given us a world inside the Psalms that is part confessional, part autobiographical, part contemplation. . . . She reveals holy moments and spiritual awakenings with delicate humor and holy levity. . . . Go on! Make yourself a pot of tea, return to that warm, cushioned place where the Spirit usually finds you, and let your soul soar through these poems."

—**Wanda Stride**, Minister, United Church of Canada

"Like a diamond, Janis holds up each psalm and turns it around and around, contemplating it, refracting each facet through the eyes of her soul, and then offering what she sees to us. Hers is an offering that takes us to places we might never have thought of going. And through it all, the depth of her faith and trust in God shines through."

—**Colin MacDonald**, retired Minister, United Church of Canada

"*Random and Nebulous—Nuancing the Psalms* is a wonderful companion for your morning meditation, a gift of contemplative exploration, a personal journey into transformation, gratitude, and the assurance of God's *Holy Lovelight*. I choose a random excerpt daily to focus my morning meditation and guide my day. I listen with intention and delight for Janis' sacred soul message."

—**Judi Shields**, retired Social Worker

Random and Nebulous— Nuancing the Psalms

Mark,

May these words
add colour to your world

Janis Constable

Random and Nebulous— Nuancing the Psalms

Voice of the Celtic Christian Contemplative Soul
in Prose and in Prayer

Janis Constable

Foreword by Colin MacDonald

RESOURCE *Publications* • Eugene, Oregon

RANDOM AND NEBULOUS—NUANCING THE PSALMS
Voice of the Celtic Christian Contemplative Soul in Prose and in Prayer

Resource Publications
An Imprint of Wipf and Stock Publishers
199 W. 8th Ave., Suite 3
Eugene, OR 97401

www.wipfandstock.com

PAPERBACK ISBN: 978-1-6667-1763-1
HARDCOVER ISBN: 978-1-6667-1764-8
EBOOK ISBN: 978-1-6667-1765-5

NOVEMBER 2, 2021

For the
decidedly discerning
spiritually savoring
poetically prayerful
contemplatively called
mystical minds—

I offer the depths of my contemplative world to you.

May you open your whole being
and deeply attune
to the words,
to the wonder,
to the wisdom.

Contents

FOREWORD

SOMEONE WISE ONCE SAID that while Scripture speaks *to us*, the Psalms speak *for us*. The landscape of our lives, its joys and struggles, can be found within the Psalms. They are eternally close to home and heart, speaking deeply to our life's journey with God, and with one another. Like the commandments of God, the Psalms are "more precious than gold, even much fine gold". (Psalm 19:10)

And while gold is an excellent image, allow me to steal from the apostle Paul in I Corinthians 12, and invite you to consider a *more* excellent image—the Psalms as a treasure of 150 diamonds. Each diamond has its own quality. Some are light and shimmering, some are dark and mysterious. Some rejoice, others lament, and at times even rage. And like every diamond, every Psalm has any number of facets through which we can see the fullness of its wonder.

While diamonds, of course, are known for their beauty, they are also known to be the hardest material on earth. Only diamond drill bits can cut through any other type of stone. And the Psalms, while filled with beauty, can be equally hard, equally able to cut, especially cut through any preconceived notions we may have about God, and our relationship with God. They can open up new facets that we might never have seen before. And they are able to etch into the human heart—even hearts of stone—images and truths that will remain.

This is what I experience when I read Janis Constable's offerings in her book, *Random and Nebulous—Nuancing the Psalms*. She has taken ten of those diamonds and held them up into what she calls the Lovelight of God. Holding each precious stone, she turns it around and around, finding the uniqueness of each facet, contemplating it, refracting each facet through the eyes of her soul, and then offering what she sees to us. She takes us to

xi

places we might never have thought of going. And through it all, the depth of her faith and trust in God shines brightly.

I have known Janis Constable as a friend for more than twenty years. I was the newly-called pastor of Central United Church in Barrie Ontario, when she and her husband Barry arrived. Into that congregational constellation, Janis brought her gifts and her life and her deep abiding faith. Through that time, I have come to know Janis as a choir member, an active member of the worship team, a hymn writer and poet, and, as a ministry colleague when she served in Parish Nursing Ministry at Central.

Professionally, Janis had been an emergency room nurse for many years at a number of hospitals in central Ontario. That part of her life was one of quick decisions and diagnoses, working with fellow medical team members to bring patients back from whatever brink at which they found themselves, fixing problems that needed fixing, even when time was not on her side. Yet, she also had a less "fixy" side—a side where contemplation took over from problem solving, and where time was not something to work against, but to allow simply to be. It is from this place of creative faith that she shares with us, delving deep into the heart of these particular Psalms. She holds them before us and invites us to ponder them, as she has done.

Now, it isn't necessary to agree with her, and I believe that, ultimately, that is not her goal. Janis' goal is to show us that Scripture is not simply black print on white page, but a living, breathing witness of God's relationship with all creation, and our relationship with God who creates, redeems and sustains all life. This is especially so—and has already been noted—as the Psalms speak *for us.* Janis invites us to see images and facets of these particular diamonds, and then to find images and facets of our own, that can speak to our hearts, and, speak into the heart of God.

I invite you to journey with Janis through these few Psalms. Through both poetry and prose, she brings out the lustre of God's love for us in Christ.

Reverend Dr. Colin MacDonald+
June 2021
Barrie, Ontario, Canada

PREFACE

IN A WORLD OF 'Hurry up and go', and 'Just put yer head down and git 'er dun!'—In a world where appetites for authority, power and control supersede the simple ways of 'being', and 'being-one-with'—In a world of noise, and whiter noise, and hum and din and drone—the spiritual practices of silence, stillness, and solitude ostensibly 'get left in the dust'. Sadly, in this pressured, hurried, crazy-busy world, they are reduced to uselessness, redundancy, and blatant obsolescence.

But, things are fortunately changing. The winds are lifting and the tides are shifting. This wounded weary world is beginning to yearn, to seek, and to re-discover *what it means to embody a balanced well-being, in body, mind and spirit. There is a conscious re-turning to the wholesome ways of olde—a re-turning to the disciplines of the heart. Becoming a beloved being or body, open to a mindful mindset, and, serving with a centered, savoring spirit—these are some of the new, yet rooted in olde, core values in the chosen and cherished contemplative life. Faith emerges as a main ingredient in the recipe of whole-person-health and wellness.* And, there is a growing individual and collective awareness and appreciation of 'interior work', in the name of becoming more/most fully human—in the name of being whole and one-with-God—in the name of sensing the Sacred deep within.

I invite you right here, right now, to engage with me, in my wonderful Celtic Christian contemplative world, where the random and nebulous become discerned and defined. Together, we'll consider ten chosen Psalms. We'll filter them, feather them, and refine them—nuancing them—only to watch fresher, simpler themes emerge. *Choose Well—Choose God/ Let God Lead/ Listen for God Deep Within/ Be Still, and Come to Know God/ Seek Forgiveness/ Rest Safely with God/ Seek God's Presence and God's Provision/ Let God Help/ Formed, Known and Loved by God/ Celebrate God*—These ten succinct synoptic chapter titles are truly transparent. They are indeed, the central heartfelt messages of David, a common-shepherd-boy-become-King who truly loved his God, from just a few thousand years ago.

The nuanced Psalm messages are not likened to watered down pablum, rather, they are indeed, a scrumptious and hearty feast! I invite you to take your time, and to slowly, slowly, savor this soul-nourishing repast. Perhaps the subtle taste and aromas of ancient Celtic Wisdom—simmered and stirred into the newly nuanced Psalmic Insight—will call out to you, awakening your own contemplative palate, drawing you in—deep and deeper.

Perhaps my personal musings will echo, or mirror, or parallel your recent reflections. Perhaps what was once 'random and nebulous' in your own tender faith, may soon become wholly 'intentional and clear'—even 'luminous and real'! I invite you to read and reflect, with eyes, ears, minds and hearts wide, wide open.

Allow my words and my wanderings to gather you in—to gather you in close—closer to God. And, lift you up. May they sweep you along and set you squarely into the realm of Holy Ground. Let them whisk you away to an extraordinary time and place—a Sacred Space—comfortably nestled in the Presence of God. May they become a novel and unique starting point, giving rise to your own impassioned questions, and queries. May you discover glistening new meaning and new perspectives—and behold sparkling epiphanies—both common and grand. May you even experience self-transcendence.

Come now, and let *Random and Nebulous* seduce your contemplative spirit, that you may attune—attune intently and intensely—to the wisdom, to the truth—to the sweet summons of the Sacred Sage of your soul.

Janis Constable

ACKNOWLEDGMENTS

To all of the Spiritual Nudges
that awakened my contemplative soul,
that encouraged me on my writing journey,
that empowered my task-driven will—

Thanks Be.

To all of the ordained and scholarly
"Saints of and Voices of
the Ancient Celtic Wisdom"
whose written and spoken words
opened my heart "to see"—

Thank you.

To my own family roots,
in the Clan Buchanan Motto—
Clarior Hinc Honos—
which inherently calls out through the ages to my soul,
to sense and to savor and to celebrate
the brightness of the Light, and Enlightenment—

So be it. Amen.

Chapter One

PSALM 1

Psalm 1 Choose Well—Choose God

In standing by the rivershore,
   I drink in all that is.
      I am strong. I want for nothing. My needs are met.
         My life has been, and is now, bearing fruit. Abundantly.

A wonderful journey has led me to this shore,
   by the fresh and sparkling waters.
      Choices came to me, at many crossroads along the way,
         and my reward is my stance, and my dance,
            at the river's edge.

Choosing this path,
   choosing this perspective,
      choosing this power of love and grace over lust and greed,
         has prospered me, provided me, and positioned me,
            in a life worthy of the great river.

May I ever and always choose well,
   that I may live strong, by the rivershore.
      Velut arbor aevo.

Thoughts

We choose to think.
   Thoughts are mere tracings of reality and dreams.
     Winks and wisps of imagination.
       Nuances of notions.
         Strung together in logical orderly patterns, or,
           erratically scattered like dandelion seeds
            in the wind.

Words and images merge into thoughts,
   as vague silhouettes
     in the fiery, random and nebulous inner workings of the mind,
       arising as freshness in the darkness
         of our center-most grey matter.

Transient, persistent, and often imperceptible nudgings
   of ethereal, mystical or spiritual origins
     are ever-stirring the mind's eye—
       to question and to contemplate—
         to formulate quasi-original streams of consciousness—
           to kindle *nouveau et beau*, brash and brazen,
             insights, visions and views.

Thoughts are the touchstones,
   the X, Y, and Z of the mysterious equations of human essence.
     And, they are the cornerstones—and the base!—
       of the pyramidal world of metaphysics.

Thoughts are born
   in the intentional and frenzied space of the creative mind,
     and often, elusively,
       out of the stillpoint,
         in the spacious-yet-centered
           Light of all life.

Thoughts stir, awaken, and begin to flow.
Thoughts twist and turn, blur and blend, bend and curve—
gandering, meandering, wandering—and then, *accelerando!* Whoa!!

Thoughts can morph into waypoints.
Thoughts can storm, and, shelter from the storm!
Thoughts can dwarf our fears, and shepherd our souls.
Thoughts forge dynamic links between
the ethereal, mystical, spiritual,
and the very real and tangible realms of daily life.
Thoughts keep us on our chosen pathway with our God.

Thoughts feed the hungry, the thirsty, and the yearning
body, mind and spirit.
Thoughts nourish and nurture and nudge us—
fully, wholesomely, deeply.

Were the brain able to breathe, thoughts would be the breath.

With prayer as your breath, make good, sound, Godly choices.
Make all of your choices thoughtfully, prayerfully.
'Think God'. Thank God.

Lovelight

The Holy Lovelight is my own poetic waxing—
  my intricately laced and laden, chosen mystical word
    for all of the gracious gifts given to me by God—
      love, joy, hope, peace, grace, wisdom, insight,
        strength, courage, encouragement, comfort, healing—Presence—
        and so much more.

Lovelight—
Warm, soft, tender.
  Nebulous, yet clear-flowing, blowing, billowing and glowing.
    Surrounding and grounding—truly astounding.
      Alluring. Assuring. Enduring.

Single-iridescent-glint or,
  vibrant-roaring-fire-dance-glister.
    Arising from within, yet gracing from beyond.
      Ever-present to me.
        Ever-present for all.

A rush of Light.
  A blush of Light.
    A hallowed, haloed, hush of Light.

A Showing.
  A Shining.
    A Shimmering.
      A Presence—
        A veritable Theophany!

Seen. Sensed. Savored.
  Intuited—and most especially, known.

Lovelight is a wholesome—and wholly experiential—gift from God.
　　Lovelight is personal and intimate,
　　　　yet broadly and radically universal.
　　　　　Lovelight is real—so tangibly, authentically real—
　　　　　　for those who are open to its spectral ubiquity—
　　　　　　　for those who are open to its Sacred Uniquity.

"There are no earthly shadows, in the Lovelight of my God". Selah

And daily I sing out the affirming words of my own
　　personal powerful yet prayerful mantra—

　　In my God I'll be ever thankful
　　　for the Lovelight graces me—
　　　　Stirring deep within my heart and soul
　　　　Leading me through all the darkness
　　　　Calling me to walk in Holiness.

Accept the gracious invitation—
　　the Lovelight-borne invitation,
　　　in the call of the Holy Lovelight—
　　　　to draw ever near, into the heart of God,
　　　　　to seek the Presence of God,
　　　　　　to be One-with-God.

Choose to let the Holy Lovelight enter—
　　into your world, into your heart, into your very depths.

Choose to live in the Light.
　　Choose to live in the wonder—in the warmth—in the mystery.
　　　Choose to live a life of pure contentment and spiritual well-being—
　　　　in the Holy Lovelight of God.

Arise, energized, internalizing this God-given gift of Light.
  Walk on your way—
    in wisdom,
      and in Holy wonder,
        and with God-with-you.
          Step out and shine brightly,
            in the Holy Lovelight of God!

Please receive my gift of modern Celtic Blessing upon you—

May you be blessed with—
  Love to warm you
    Light to lead you
      And God's Holy Lovelight
        to hold and keep you—
          For now and always—
            Amen.

Linger long in Lovelight. Selah

Patrick's Plate

He was wrenched from his homeland, held in captivity,
  and sent out to shepherd, to slave in the fields.
    The early Christian teachings had already nestled into his heart,
      and this gave him hope, and strength, and firmed up his faith.

He had visions and dreams,
  and always found ways and means,
    to learn, to discern, and to grow.

Starving and hungry, he was fed by his faith.
  He hungered for the Word.
    He thirsted for knowledge and understanding.
      He listened.
        He shared what he learned.
        Patrick's life was full.
        Patrick's plate was full.

As 'Voice of the Irish', as Bishop,
  he chose—he arose—to rise up and to serve.
    His passion and purpose were perfected in prose.

From slave-boy to Saint, he grew into *great*.

We can all choose, like Patrick.
  Choose faith.
    Choose to step up and to answer the call.
      Choose to persevere through the darkness and the storms.
      Choose to reach out to every, and to all.

We won't all be Sainted, or earn a parade,
  but, with a Servant Heart,
    we will serve God—and live out our faith.
    And our plates too—shall be full.

Choosing the Realm of Liminality

Realm of Liminality
  is a transitional time
    between the old and the new,
      where the old order is lost
        and the new transformation has not yet begun.
          It is found, balanced on the threshold of change.

Liminality is a time of fresh malleability, and readiness.

In my emergence as a Celtic Christian,
  I have chosen to enter into the Realm of Liminality,
    as I re-open my eyes, my ears, and my heart,
      to 'the way of seeing'—
        to that with which I was originally born.

My eager and ready and optimistic transformation
  is energized from a deep yearning to acknowledge
    the true soul that I am.
      And indeed that is a beloved child of God,
        called to serve in Christ-like living.

On my quiet quest into Holiness-and-Christ-like-Living,
  I have entered into the Liminal Realm of Transformation,
    and into the Realm of Liminal Thinking.

And I choose to look deep within me, to the very centre of my being,
  for inner wisdom, insight and guidance,
    in the re-shaping and the re-turning of my faith, my heart, and my all.

I choose to listen to, and to attune to,
  the Voices of the Ancient Celtic Wisdom
    that bring me to new doorways
      and to new thresholds
        of my tender Living Faith.

I also choose to turn to the writings of the Spiritual Masters,
  whose deep faith and critical thinking and contemplative journeys
    guide me in my ongoing spiritual formation and transformation.

My life is a string of lovely lustrous Liminal Pearls which 'grace me'.
  My Liminal Moments 'grace me' with their special place—
    Liminal Places and Spaces—
      which are fresh, new, boundless—and real.

My time in the Realm of Liminality
  is my own personal greening time,
    and my own personal greening space—
      a choice made by me, for me.
        To be free to make such life-changing choices
          is both an honor and a privilege.

May I ever and always, choose so well.
  May I emerge in Liminal Grace. Selah

My Faith Identity

I have worshipped in the United Church of Canada all of my life,
yet, I identify with and I choose to commune with
the saints and the living saints of Celtic Christianity.

The Celtic 'way of seeing',
and their 'way of listening and hearing'
are intrinsically the way of my heart,
the way of my faith,
the way of my spiritual life,
the way of my whole life.

The ancient Celtic expression of unity and oneness with God,
is my song,
and I am ever singing,
ever chanting,
ever rising up with my song.

My chosen personal journey
into the music and the poetry of the Holy Lovelight
has grounded me,
has greened me,
and, has graced me.
The Holy Lovelight is alive in me
and it's there for me to share with others—
to kindle and ignite the Joy of Living Faith
in all whom I meet.

God is with me. I am One-with-God.
  And I am whole, and peaceful and contented,
    in this understanding—
      in this truth.

As the River flows,
  and as the Lovelight grows,
    let me always choose God.
      Let my heart always 'see the Sacred in all that lives'.
        Let me sing my song.
          Let me shine my Light—
            the Holy Lovelight of God.

Dear God,
  Let all of my good choices
    allow my tender new identity to emerge,
      that I might serve You—
        and serve You well! Amen!

My Transcendence

I chose to step away
  from my knowledge and my books and my higher learning.
    With no fears, or qualms—
      and, undaunted in my intrepid resolve—
        I stepped over the threshold into the liminal space,
          and into the spaciousness of the spiritual realm.

I was led there,
  drawn there,
    called there,
      when it was clear that I was ready, open,
        and completely surrendered and humble enough to do so.
          I didn't see this clearly then,
            but it is so crystal clear to me now.

I stepped out of rigidity, and rules and doctrine,
  and found myself in an experiential landscape
    of ancient wisdom, truth, Sacredness, grace, Agape Love—
      and Light.
        It was so naturally breezy and fresh and exhilarating—
          and inviting.
            The sound of the Eternal
              resonated deeply within me,
                and connected me
                  to what I felt was home.
                    My home.
                      My spiritual home.

I felt welcomed home.
    And in this Thin Place—
        this connection—
            this connectedness—
                this interconnectedness felt so good,
                    so real, so very right for me.

I stood tall, eager, hopeful, and full of anticipation.
    The boundaries and limits of time slipped away
        as I entered into wholeness and into oneness
            in my humble spiritual awakening.
                Expansiveness was no longer just a word.
                I was 'living it' right there and then.

I knew in my heart that I was changing.
    Not growing. Not evolving. Not transforming.
        But clearly, I was transcending.

In the freshness, in the newness, in the Light, in the Presence,
    I moved beyond the domain of my own body mind and spirit.
        I crossed over the shimmering waters into an incredible space—
        a grand river of both ancient and contemporary truth,
            churning with currents
                of conceptually concurrent
                    wisdom and truth,
                        all flowing clean, and fast and free.

I could see so clearly.
    My thoughts were simple and logical and organized.
        I could actually see with my heart, and feel with my mind.

I was walking on Holy Ground,
    sensing a certain grounded-ness,
        yet, I felt that I was ethereally floating there in the Lovelight—
            in the Holy Lovelight of God.
                I felt blessed. I *was* blessed.

I've been a different person ever since.
   I am comfortably calm, and contented, and centered.
      I'm, still 'unpacking my transcendence'
         layer by layer,
            scene by scene,
               sight by sight,
                  nuance by nuance.

I know that for me, the spiritual realm is truly a tangible thing.
   I look forward to more time spent in transcendence.
      I'm grateful to have been graced by God,
         and I'm ready to be called again by God,
            to the ancient river of wisdom and truth,
               into the Presence,
                  into the Lovelight,
                     into the timely treasure of transcendence.
                  I'm ready to step into the Light.
                     Let it be so.

My Heart

My heart is a cradle, for the love of God
  gently and tenderly—keeping.

My heart is a lantern, for the Light of God
  warmly and brightly—leading.

My heart is a harbor, for the peace of God
  safely and surely—sheltering.

My heart is a river, for the grace of God
  constantly and fervently—flowing.

My heart is a mountain, with the power of God
  truly and openly—strengthening.

My heart is a mirror, being one-with-God
  luminous, reflective—serving.

My heart is Peniel—face-to-face-with-God
  faithfully and humbly—choosing.

Choose Play

Jump. Run. Shriek and squeal. Giggle. Guffaw. Sing. Shout. Share.
  Dance. Free dance. Interpretive body dance.
    Imaginary dance partner. Imaginary friend.
      Interpose yourself in a paired fantasy dance.
        Reckless abandon of movement
          and passionate expression.

Whirl. Twirl. Swing. Dip. Embrace. Hold.
  Back to reality.

Kick. Throw. Toss. Volley. Spike. Stickhandle.
  Skate. Skate backwards. Dare to close your eyes!
    Cartwheel. Somersault. Aerial somersault.
      Stride. Quicken your stride. Stride out.

Daydream. Imagine. Confabulate.
  Invent a game, and make your own game rules.
    Play it.
      Teach it to your play pals.
        You have none?
          Find some.
            Seek some.
              Imagine them,
                and then
                  play hide and seek!

Create. Re-create. Invent. Re-invent. Design. Re-design.

Play, in each of the body, mind and spirit realms.
  Games and sports are fun for the body.
    Use mind games, brain twisters and tongue twisters,
      fog-lifters and brain-drain-stumpers
        to keep your brain healthy.

Then move on to the spiritual games—
　　spiritual gifts, spiritual disciplines—
　　　　and try some deep-core-centering-spiritual-and-interior-workouts,
　　　　　　where 'alive happens' on the inside!

In everything, play.
　　In every time, play.
　　　　In every season, play.
　　　　　　In every realm, play.

Play for fun, and play for joy. Play with energy, and *joie de vivre.*
　　Play, with God as your coach, your mentor, your inspiration—
　　　　your Light.
　　　　　　Choose play, and truly feel alive—vibrant and free.

Play is so very therapeutic, at so many levels.
　　Play is downright under-rated.
　　　　Have you exercised your body, mind and spirit today?
　　　　　　Have you simply played today?
　　　　　　　　Choose to just let yourself go, and play. Selah

Choose Joy

Joy is an elevated and excited state of being.
It's more than a happy heart or a broad grinning moment,
or a hand-clappin'-foot-stompin'-vocal-cheering-chorus.

Joy is an energy,
an inherent undulating waveform spreading warmth—
in ripples of happiness, smiles, and laughter,
and in auras of contentment and well-being.

The energy of joy manifests easily,
in lightheartedness, in spontaneous chatter and song,
in erupting exuberance, friendliness, and openness,
and in the dropping of guard and boundaries.

The power of joy is limitless,
boundless, and inherently unbridled.

Choosing to let joy energize you,
empower you, and free you,
is a humbling thing.

No one was ever jailed for joy.
If they were persecuted for joy,
they were more than likely
misunderstood and mistaken,
as being unruly and roisterous and rogue,
by the staid and stiff and unyielding
jealous law-makers of the time.

Choose to let joy overcome you,
and to let it settle in to your bones.
Let joy permeate,
infiltrate and infuse
your body, mind and spirit.

Let joy become your own natural rhythm,
   your new middle name,
      your unique identifier,
         your will, your very breath.

Let joy breathe into you, that you may arise and live out your life
   in a heart-bursting and impassioned realm
      of whole-person-contentment-and-bliss.

Let joy radiate, emanate, and shine from deep within your being.

Sing out from the bottom of your heart—sing with joy!
   Sing of your inborn sparkling Light!
      No innuendo here. Simply pure ebullience and euphoria!
         Your heart beats with joy!
            Sing out until your heart becomes the joy!!!
               Sing 'My heart is joy!'—'Joy Joy Joy!'
                  So be it, for now and always, I pray!!!'

Choose God. Choose Joy. Be Joy. Amen.

Choose Hope

Hope can be—
    A breath of fresh air in a stagnant story or stand-off.
      A warm and filtered ray of sunlight in the deepest caverns of life.
        A single twinkling star in the vacuum and in the vastness
          of the navy blue night sky.
            A bonfire blazing.

Hope is also—
    A mesmerizingly colorful and energized frame of mind.
      A wholesome and positive outlook.
        A veritable compass of the heart and soul.
          True North for the weary and worn.
            A driving force in the darkness.
              An emotional gear, that when engaged,
                allows for smoother rides
                  on bumpier, rougher roads.

Hope can actually be a choice.
    Not choosing Hope leads to despair, dark holes, and deep deep pits.
    Choosing Hope 'glides you' through all life and all time—
      as do the *glissade* and *grand jeté* in the grand ballet of life.

Hope sees a heavenly haven on the horizon,
    from within the horrors and the upheavals of hell here on earth.

Hope is intangible,
    yet, it becomes something very real to hold onto fiercely,
      when faced with the frenzy of fear of the unknown.

Hope is a gift to be shared—
    a gift that is genuinely welcomed and appreciated.
      One can live vicariously through the Hope of a friend,
      when it seems that all Hope has been lost.

Indeed, Hope can be lost, but most importantly, Hope can be found.
   Hope can still be found,
      long after the lacrimal glands and sacs have all run dry.

Hope arises with conviction from the depths,
   when faith-roots run deep,
      and when trust in the Divine is truly instinctive and profound.
         The unconditional love of God
            blesses the open and receptive heart
               with "a peace that passes all understanding",[1]
                  and with a Hope
                     that dwells in the deepest well of the soul.

Hope is real. Hope heals. Hope leads from darkness into Light.
   Blessed be the Hope that glows softly—
      yet sparkles brilliantly—
         with the Holy Lovelight of God.

In the muck and the mire and the mud,
   and in all of the misery-pits of life,
      choose well.
         Choose God. Choose Hope. Amen.

1. NRSV Phil 4: 7

Vignette—Choosing Well

I chose to pack up at age 25,
    and move east to Newfoundland, Canada,
        for the job of a lifetime.

I chose to return to school, back to Ontario, for Nursing.
    Upon graduation and registration, I chose to work in Emergency,
        a choice that would give me a 33 year career,
        full of personally fulfilling and meaningful work.

I chose to write a vast collection of songs and prayers,
    detailing my life in the poetic, yet very real Holy Lovelight of God.

In my 50's, I chose to return to school
    for a late career move into Parish Nursing Ministry,
        which led me on a 10 year journey of whole-person-nursing,
        opening the door for me
            to incorporate my faith and wisdom
          in my daily work
            with patients and their families
               in my church and community.

I chose to study the Ancient Celtic Wisdom
    and to embody the simple truths of their wonderful faith tradition.

I chose to study and discern my place
    in the realm of Spiritual Direction.

I chose to write, and to become an author,
    to share in story, song and prayer,
        all the wonders of my faith journey and my spiritual journey.

Prior to each choice,
   I was given a subtle nudge,
      or an overtly plainspoken call,
         or a gift of an opportunity that appeared out of nowhere.

It was truly up to me to be open and receptive,
   discerning and decisive,
      and calm and courageous,
         to move forward and make some amazing choices
         for my life journey.

I am one strong and sturdy tree,
   firmly rooted in the nourishing earthy soils by the rivershore.
      I've grown a massive root system, and trunk and branches,
         and I have produced much shade and fruit over the years.

My life presented me
   with so many crossroads, chances, and opportunities,
      and I stood tall and answered the call,
         and I am richly rewarded by my God, God-with-me,
         God-within-me.

I affirm that I am 'born of God', and all created life is also 'born of God'.
   I see all life as Holy, Sacred, and this relational perspective
      allows me to show respect, to be compassionate,
         and to serve with a loving and generous heart.
      I see the Sacred in all that lives.

I choose this heartset, mindset, soulset, and faithset,
   and consequently, my faith journey and life journey have now merged
      into one grand odyssey of love.

I will continue to choose, choose well, choose God,
   as I approach life, and 'see all life' with the eyes of my heart.

Choosing God has led me to a life that is abundant indeed.
And, just like the Psalmist's tree—David's Tree—
which grows by the waters edge,
I am flourishing. Life is good.
Thanks be to God.

Prayer Based on Psalm 1

In living out my faith, in the Contemplative Life,
  with an inborn yearning for truth,
    may I always make choices that keep me on the right path—
      that help me to grow like a sturdy tree
        planted by the water's edge.
          May all the choices I make
            bring me closer to You, oh God.

May the fruits of Jan's Tree—of my tree—of my faith,
  strengthen me and prosper me,
    that I may do the work I'm called to do.
      May I delight in Your Word and in Your Works,
        and, may I ever share the joy of my Living Faith
        with all whom I meet.

Please hold me,
  please nurture me by the rivershore,
    please watch over me, I pray. Amen.

CHAPTER TWO

PSALM 23

Psalm 23 Let God Lead

The Kindest Shepherd is my Gentle Pastor.
With Him, I want for nothing at all.
I'll seek and search no more.
He makes sure that I rest.
He shows me the warmth
of His peace and calm.
He brings Light to my soul.

His Holy Lovelight stills me, heals me,
and makes me whole.
He tells me His way,
and I choose the right paths on my journeys.

And in the depths, in the darkest times of my journey,
I'll not be afraid,
nor will I worry.
For You God, my Kindest Shepherd, are with me.
Your very Presence brings me comfort.
You quiet my restless heart.

You raise me up amidst the unbelievers.
You freely give to me.
You gift me with the wonders of Your abundance
and Your blessings.

I believe that Your loving-kindness will grace me,
in Your Holy Lovelight,
through all my earthly days.

And I will walk with You, my Gentle Pastor,
hand in hand, heart in heart,
one with You forever.
I will journey in the Living Faith
in Your Holy Lovelight, forever.
Amen.

Oh Still Small Voice

Oh "Still Small Voice",[1]
  You call my heart
    You urge my feet
      to venture along
        to journey ahead—

Across the waters
  beyond the islands
    on top of the mountains
      and through the storms
        around the bends
          and the curves
            and the twists
              and the cliffs.

To 'river on'
  into the Light
    into the deep
      onto my knees
        through the dark
          through the night
            through the pain
              through the loneliness.

To the joy
  to the peace
    to the hope
      to Your Unconditional Love.

Encouraging my love
  and my faithfulness
    and my surrender,
      now and always.

1 NKJV 1 Kings 19: 12

Oh Still Small Voice[2]
  I hear You
    and I am listening
      with all my heart.
        Trusting in Your Promise—
          Trusting in Your Presence—
          Wherever You lead.
          Amen.

2 NKJV 1 Kings 19: 12

So Much More Than a Poem

Open my eyes on the Columba Shores
  and let me bask in the later-day sun,
    communing with earth, and the sea and the sky—
    Open my eyes 'to see more'.

Open my heart on the Columba Shores
  I take in the ancient, the present, the now.
    Eternity roves on the rocks and the beach—
    Stirring my heart 'to see more'.

Open my faith on the Columba shores
  attuning my depths to the wisdom and truth.
    Music-of-the-spheres rises in great-voiceless-words—
    Calling my faith 'to see more'.

God of my heart on the Columba Shores
  I open to wholeness in Holy Lovelight
    Your Light and my Light connecting within—
    Together as One, 'we are more'.

      Chant. Repeat. Pray—
        Together as One—on the shore—
          Together as One—'we are more'—
        Selah

Who Dries My Tears

When all that I am
　　and all that is me
　　　　is dark and empty and grievously painful,
　　　　　　I want a God who weeps with me.

But, more than this—
　　I want a God who dries my tears
　　　　and who leads me out of my darkness,
　　　　　　and who walks with me
　　　　　　　　into His glorious Light.

All thanks be to my God,
　　the God of grace,
　　　　the God of unconditional love,
　　　　　　the God of compassion and forgiveness,
　　　　　　　　the God of Perfect Peace,
　　　　　　　　　　the God of hope and Eternal Light—
　　　　　　　　　　the God who lights me and leads me
　　　　　　　　　　in Holy Lovelight.
　　　　　　　　　　　　Amen.

Through the Marmalade—Finding Clarity

Many, many original recipes and variations on a theme.
  4-H First Prize Ribbons, Grand Champions,
    and Judge's Choice award winners,
      are mostly bittersweet, always congealed, and truly a tasty mix!
    Marmalades invariably have an 'it factor'
      in the spectrums of clarity and lucence—
        Opaque, Translucent, Semi-Translucent,
        and occasionally,
          Clearly Transparent!

Marmaladen textured and twisted ingredients
  are boiled and simmered and boiled again.
    Then they land in clear-glass Mason jars,
      random and nebulous where they thicken and set,
        together as one.

A simple spoon or spreading knife,
  can alter the spatial relationship
    of the preserved marmalade ingredients.
      And, it can separate them into smaller,
        yet, still scrumptious portions.

So too, can the Contemplative, the Mystic, and the Sage,
  take on the random and nebulous wisdom and truths,
    and delight in the inherent depths.
      They choose to taste—savor—
        the relevance and meaning, and the wonder within.

In Newtonian language,
  Marmalade's own haphazard chaos and inertia,
    can be scattered and spread and shared,
      widely, broadly, intensely,
        by external unbalanced predictable forces!

In McLuhanian language,
  The Medium of Marmalade is the message.
    And the Message is the Medium of Marmalade!

And in cryptic, curving Constabilian contemplation—
  The 'Spirit of the Marmalade'
    will always remain intact, unbroken, inseparable.
  The 'Soul of Marmalade'—whole and one.

Gaze deeply into your gifts of Marmalade—
  sticky bitter zest and all.
    Dare to dwell in the seeming frozen frenzy, 'Marmalades of Life'.
    Seek them. Ponder them.
      Know them. Cherish them.
      Live them. Love them.
      Learn from them.

Allow your savvy sage self to taste, to experience, and to be led—
  into 'Marmalade Moments',
    and into 'Marmalade Musings'.
      Find yourself in the 'Marmalade of Wonderment'.
      Whet your appetite for
        the wholesome and hearty,
          the comforting and completing,
          the memorable and mystical.

These are all deliciously discernable
  in the Contemplative's own
    curious palate and plate of life.

When God gives you Marmalade—
  Assapora la Marmaletta di Dio!!!
    Savor—Savor—Savor!!!
      Selah

Bereft

Drifting. Despairing. Painfully or recklessly abandoned.
Slowly, in a tortuous and torturous demise of the soul.
Disconnected. Unfriended. Separated.
Food is tasteless. Fun doesn't exist.

Friends don't exist.
Friends are unable to comprehend,
articulate, or encourage.
They fade away, withdraw, withhold,
in the wake of their own fears,
ineptitudes, and seeming helplessness.

Grief weighing heavy.
Anguish as an anchor pulling down.
Angst as an aching.
Lament circling the consciousness
like a gaudy lavish laurel wreath.

The only Light in the depths of darkness is God.
Always with. Always present. Always within.
God weeps—and God weeps some more.
God walks with. God holds and embraces.

God carries the bereaving and the lost
over the dark and roiling, unruly and unordered waters.
Out of the dark and into the Light—
onto the shores "beside the still waters".[1]

God never leaves.
God never forsakes.
God never leaves us bruised, broken or bereft.
We are never alone. Never, ever, ever.
God is with us—
Thanks be to God. Amen.

1. NRSV Ps 23: 2

38

Oh God, My Blessed Living God

Oh God my blessed living God
in my humble heart I know
You will lead me to the water's edge
where the peaceful waters flow.
When my wandering spirit soars
bring me home, my faith restore.
Take my hand and let me walk with You
in a world of grace and truth.

As I walk in darkened valleys God
my fears I will overcome.
You will journey with me in my heart
Comfort me Almighty One!
And I know You'll stand by me
I am blessed abundantly!
Your love completes me, makes me whole,
You enrich my very soul.

Oh God forgive me all my days
Your compassion will set me free.
Oh God of tender mercy grant
Eternal Love for me.
Oh God my living God!
Oh Creator, Holy Word!
Keep me in Your blessed love and care
Dear God please hear my prayer.

Brigid's Motherfire

Brigid's Light, Eternal Light, her story warms my heart.
She welcomed. She healed. She fed.
She nourished. She nurtured. She led.

Brigid herself was said to be born in the 'twilight of the dawn'.
With two grand lights shining in the same great sky—
with the sun and moon both courting the earth at her birth—
it is right that her name-full-of-Light means
'Shining One', 'Great One', 'Shining Deep Within'.

How tender the ancient Celtic tenet, that the woman of the household
should tend the 'mother-fire' in the home—in the hearth—
that her family be warm
that her family be safe
that her family would be
in the Light—of the Light—
that they themselves would become
the brightly shining Lights.
The hearthfire should never,
ever, go out.

It's no wonder that I am drawn to Brigid, St Brigid of Kildare.
Long before the mystical St John wrote
"The Light shines in the darkness
and the darkness did not overcome it", [1]
she embodied Light, and Light emanated from her—
the Sacred Inner Light.

As a strong and centered woman,
she understood what it was to be
of the Light,
graced by the Light—
Living in the Light.

1. NRSV John 1: 5

The Holy Lovelight is ever near, and ever dear to me.
I sense it. I savor it. And I celebrate it.
And with it, my own tender Light stirs into flame,
enlivened, and flickering up into fire!
And I humbly thank God
as the Holy Lovelight ever-graces me.

Thank you Brigid for sharing your Light,
your mothering, your mentoring,
and your deep, deeper and deepest meaning.
May your Eternal Light and 'motherfire'
illumine, and lift, and liberate—
and shine strong and bright
for all the world to see.

I am sparked by St Brigid
Lured by the Light
Led by the Shepherd
to Holy Lovelight.

Vignette—My Word

It was a September canoe trip, at day's end.
  Dinner and dishes were done,
    and food was safely stowed away for the overnight.

The campfire was down by the shore,
  and its lingering embers were quivering with radiant heat.
    I'd had an adventurous and exhilarating day
      out on the great 'Temagami Blue' waters,
        and now it was so easy to kick back, relax,
          and drift into, and away, and along—
            in a welcomed
              and deeply contemplative sit.

Feeling safe, secure, centered and strong,
  I looked up, away from the glowing embers.
    Up, up, up to the matrix of celestial bodies shining brightly.
      They were so many light-years away
        from my humble-here-and-now.

Then the magic began!
  Columns and seeming waves of ethereal dancing light
    graced the heavenly heights.
      Patterns and no patterns.
        Rhythm and no rhythm.
          Symmetry and chaos.
            Neon and pastels.

Even my own breathy and exaggerated ooooohs and ahhhhhs!

The Canadian Aurora Borealis descended upon me,
  lavishly adorning me with Light,
    in layers of mystery, mystique and magnificence.

My own spaciousness grew.
My personal sense of expansiveness broadened.
My mind's doorway to openness and receptivity
was flung open wide,
revealing a grand celestial stage
for my impending Holy Moment.

In my wide-eyed state of transcendent liminality,
I was given—a word.
This was a spoken word, yet, it was voiceless.
I heard it from within me—*and from beyond.*
It was spoken calmly, clearly stated,
and, it was truly comprehensible.

The deep rich tone reverberated in my depths,
and the meaning and the implications of this word
resonated deeply in my soul.
This single blessed word arose in a Holy Moment,
through the truth of the ages,
and through the wisdom of all eternity.
It was shown, and then known,
and then owned, by me.

God gave me a word that has changed my life.
He led me safely on my journey,
and made me rest by the still starlit waters.

And then He spoke into my heart 'the word'
that would lead me through
the darkened valleys
and up to the mountain tops.

Symbolically, that word would be with me,
as God would be with me, all my days.
Most surely, I would walk with God and be led by God,
for always and forever.
Thanks be to God for the word. My word.

+++

God gifted me with the preciously profound and purely poetic word —
'Lovelight'.
And, not only am I graced by the Holy Lovelight—
I am traipsing in, transforming in, and transcending in
The Holy Lovelight of God.
I was born of the Light,
and I have spent all of my adult life, living in the Light—
The Holy Lovelight of God.
In the wonders of the Lovelight,
my heart sings out in praise to God—
Hallelujah!
My faith becomes alive and real—
in the Holy Lovelight of God!
Amen!!!

Prayer Based on Psalm 23

I find comfort.
  I am contented.
    I am calm in the leading of the Shepherd.
      I trust that wherever I am led,
        I will be safe,
          my heart will be at ease,
            and that I will be strong
              in knowing of God's Presence
              and of God's leading.

Down the road, through the darkness,
  on the precipice, in the swamps,
    and in the Liminal Space of the threshold,
      God will lead me,
        and I will carry God in my heart
          in all my ways, in all my days.

I live, I grow, and I rest
  in the assurance of
    and in the wonder of
      the Presence of God—
        the oneness of God—
          and God-with-me.
            Amen.

CHAPTER THREE

PSALM 42

Psalm 42 Listen for God Deep Within

Come into God's Presence
    with a carefree centering calm, and serenity,
        and stay there awhile!
            Let "Deep call to Deep"[1]!

Listen. Be. Listen some more.
    Then enter a heartfelt prayer
        asking God to lead you, to guide you—
            asking God to show you the way.

Pray for whatever transformative healing you need from God,
    to follow in His new path for you.
        Pray for strength and courage for the journey.

In your prayer, go deep
    and call out to God.
        When "Deep calls to Deep"[2]
            God touches you deep in your soul.
                Seek this.
                    Sense this.
                    Savor this.

1. paraphrase of NRSV Ps 42: 7
2. NRSV Ps 42: 7

Time

Time—lingering and laboring.
   Washing over, wafting, waffling, wasting,
      willowing, whiling, whirling.

A standstill at sunrise,
   yet riding with rivers
      and strutting in storms.

Suspended in sunsets. Soliciting sleep.

It meticulously metered and measured the past.
   But real-time-in-the-now, here and now,
      is shaping and shoring the present,
         and foreshadowing
            all of the days that are yet to come.

Reckless and reserved.
   Wanton and willful.
      Shamelessly sure.
         Friend. Lover. Colleague. And foe.

Life grooves as time moves.
   Dancing in perpetuity, into infinity and beyond.
   God calls through eternity.

And, at the right time, "Deep calls to Deep".[1] Selah

---

1. NRSV Ps 42: 7

Poetry

In the stillness, in the hush,
  in the moment before my next breath,
    I pause, in wonder, in awe.
      I'm simply present.

In the delight of my here and now,
  rests a poem.
    Not poetry in motion.
    Not ongoing.
      Right here,
        right now,
          is a poetic moment.
            Followed by another.
          Each is unique
          onto itself.

Looking back over time,
  recalling people, places, thoughts,
    memories arise and float and merge together
    into the poetry of my life.

Rhythms, rhymes, cadences,
  dark words, real words,
    hard words, and feathered words,
      flow into passages—
        into virtual images—
          and into my lyrical prose.

Still here, in the curve of quiescence,
  in the sway of the moment,
    my soul waxes poetic,
      in the depths,
        in the Lovelight,
          in the sweet serenity of now.
        The Poet and I are One.

Space

My soul wandered into the Lovelit space,
  and tried to know its form.
    My soul bent and curved and twisted to fit,
      but the space was simply, just there.

It tried warming, and chilling,
  but the space remained unchanged, un-moved,
    just the same.

It called out to the music of the spheres,
  but sadly,
    the earnest echoes sank swiftly, silently,
      and fell down hard to the ground.

In that space,
  my soul yearned to know
    the very essence, the centre, the core,
      the Holy Lovelight Source.

So, my soul bowed in humble, reverent prayer.
  And there, in the depths of the moment—
    in that very space in the Lovelight—
      became One.

To Wonder

An invitation—

to eagerly visit the unique, the *nouveau*, the strange,
   to sidestep or segue, and shuffle and swing,
      into the power of the muse
         to entertain possibilities and impossibilities alike.

to question broadly, freely, intently,
   to radically fantasize and confabulate in the gaps,
      in the unknown, in the mystique.

to visualize fully without necessarily comprehending,
   to simply be open 'to see'
      to yearn, to quest,
         to dream with reckless abandon,
         and with random
           and insatiable lustful desire.

to choose to dwell in mindful appreciation.
   to drift and to willfully lose track
      of time, person and place,
         while attuning deeply to the curious—
           in the whorl and the bevel,
              in the smolder and the smoke,
              in the embers
                and in the curves of the night.

to acknowledge that "Deep does call to Deep"[1]
   in the realm of Holy Lovelight.

1. paraphrase of NRSV Ps 42: 7

Blessed be the heart of wonder!
Blessed be the call of the Holy Lovelight!
Blessed be the grace and the mystery—
of wonder.
Amen.

Wonderlust

Wonderlust—real or virtual?—
  is our awe and fascination
    with the boundless beauty of
      and the unpredictability of
        nature's enduring mysteries.

Wonderlust captures our thirst
  for knowledge and things and thoughts
    beyond our understanding.

Wonderlust re-enchants us
  with fantasy and mystery,
    with play and space,
      with the novel and natural,
        with spirituality and eternity.
          It has a mystical way of casting
            both mega and mini spells
              of hope, joy, peace and contentment
                on the happy wonderer.

Blissfully-lost-in-Wonderlust is a really good thing!

Wonderlust is inborn,
  yet, it can be cultivated, even harnessed,
    into a lifestyle, an energy—
      a drive, and a *joie de vivre*—
        into an impassioned persona.

Wander intentionally into wayfaring wonderlust!
  Find your own select and unique life-experience-blessings,
    as you discover and live out
      the awesome Wonderlust in you!

Listen for the call from the Deep—
 Unleash your inner beast of Wonderlust!
  Arise and dance and play
   in the freeing rhythms of Wonderlust!
    Rise up in your restlessness,
     and revel in unrestrained Wonderlust!!!

Respond to the call from the Deep—
 opening yourself freely—becoming delightfully disinhibited
  in your thoughts and perspectives and pursuits.
   No boxes. No boundaries. No preconceived bunk.
   Only questions, queries, and quests
    on which to ponder—to wonder—
     to confabulate, extrapolate and glean.

See what unfolds for you—
 See what is revealed to you—
  See what becomes real for you—
   while 'living out loud' in Wonderlust!

Vow to expand your horizons and to grow your contemplative world.
 Entertain, epitomize, and embody Wonderlust!
  Be Wonderlust!
   Selah

Heart of Gratitude

As a tiny toddler, in her Terrible Twos,
  she was taught to say 'Please' and 'Thank You'.
  The words 'Thank You' always came easier,
    because with them came a really good feeling inside.

A warm, happy, uplifted feeling arose inside her,
  as she expressed her glee
    for whatever life-gifts had just been bestowed on her.
    That feeling made her smile.
    It made her heart smile.
      'Thank You' was truly a comfortable expression
      of the sweet emotions of her heart.

As she grew older,
  she learned a few bible phrases and poetic expressions along the way,
    that invariably made a warm interior goodness
    course through her whole being.
      Stirring titles of oldie-goldie church hymns
      would drift into her consciousness,
        and she would feel
          that rich blessedness and assurance within.

She noticed too, that lyrics of some newer popular songs
  also painted beautiful images of thankfulness, and praise.
    The contemporary 'fresh lyrics' deeply moved her—
    literally lifting her up—raising her up, and up, and up.

The clearly impassioned secular songs
  bridged her soul with their timeless message,
    evoking a powerful-and-all-encompassing-
      warming-through-and-through sensation,
        with echoes of thankfulness resounding, and resonating—
        in the deep deep well of her being.

In her thirties,
　　she heard a gently whispered whiff of a word inside her head—
　　　'Gratitude'.

"That's it!" she called out. "That's the word!
　　Gratitude is not just a plain old word anymore to me!
　　　Gratitude is an experiential thing—
　　　　Gratitude is truly a state of being—
　　　　　Gratitude is a state of heart—
　　　　　　Gratitude is a way of life, and I can say most surely
　　　　　　　that I live a Life of Gratitude—
　　　　　　　　and that my own heart is indeed
　　　　　　　　　a Heart of Gratitude!"

"And this feels really good.
　　All along I sensed there was something special happening inside
　　　when I'd say 'Thank You'.
　　　　And I know now that that warm fuzzy feeling I get,
　　　　　is truly my Heart of Gratitude
　　　　　　singing out and speaking out
　　　　　　　its perfect pleasure and delight!"

"Thanks be to my parents and to the elders in my life,
　　who took the time to teach me to say thanks,
　　　and to give thanks, and to show thanks."

"They planted the seeds for my Heart of Gratitude
　　to grow and to evolve into the
　　　beautiful-bubbling-over-larger-than-life-matter that it has become.
　　　　They set me squarely on the path
　　　　　that led me directly into the Life of Gratitude
　　　　　　that I now live, and appreciate."

"Gratitude simmers and bubbles and arises within me, always.
   And I choose to express my gratitude
      in both seen and unseen ways, through all my days.
         My heart of Gratitude is full, and rich, and soaring
            in my own colorful and abundant world".

And for this, she called out in her own exuberant and vibrant voice—
   "Thanks be! May I be thoughtful enough and strong enough
      to lead others to appreciate all of the wonders of Gratitude,
         and for them to then
            embody Gratitude in their own beautiful worlds".

And she prayed
   "May they aspire to nurture their own Heart of Gratitude,
      as they walk their own journey, in their Life of Gratitude.
         And it all starts with a simple and heartfelt—Thank You!
            Amen."

Musing on Prayer—One

To pray is to speak—
　heart to heart
　　soul to soul
　　　Light to Light
　　　　Deep to Deep
　　　　with God—

with a voice of conviction,
　and words grounded deeply in the faith,
　　with a heart full of grace,
　　　and being ever so mindful
　　　　of the spaciousness of openness,
　　　　　and the unity of Oneness—
　　　　　　of the humility of complete surrender.

Insodoing,
　this prayerful-Holy-Moment-of-God-with-you
　is the richest gift and blessing of all.

Musing on Prayer—Two

To pray is for us to stand intentionally naked before God,
    stripped of all our worldly want and zeal,
        undressed to unveil
            our absolutely bare and vulnerable selves.

Yet still,
    we stand up straight, tall, upright, fully aware, alive and present,
      clothed in the riches of God's love and grace,
        warmed by God's Holy Lovelight.

And we wait patiently to be draped—
    in an intimate, honorary cloaking ceremony—
        to be enrobed in God's welcomed Presence in our lives—
      in our attentive, attending, listening hearts.

Musing on Prayer—Three

Prayer—
   Where Humanity meets Divinity,
     where conversations are Sacred,
      where the moments are Holy,
       where the Holy Lovelight
        lightens and brightens and leads,
       where the welcomed
         "Still-Small-Voice"[1]-Whisper
        is heard clearly,
         and understood.

Where the "peace that passes all understanding"[2] is shared.
   Where the grace of God and the love of God
     flow boundlessly, freely, and unconditionally.
     Where peace, grace and love connect to the Holy.

Prayer is an invitation into intimate Oneness with God.
   Accept the invitation,
     and approach with honesty and humility and unwavering trust.
     Pray without limits, without fears, without regret.

May God's Holy Lovelight warm your heart,
   as you enter into the heart of God, through prayer.

1. NKJV 1 Kings 19: 12
2. NRSV Phil 4: 7

Amen

An exquisitely unique word of grace
   which so very comfortably finds its own niche,
      nestled in the realm of prayer and praise.

A word that takes on an unequivocal humility—
   an earthiness and a growing groundedness—
      and a sweet simplicity all of its own.

It first descends
   only then to ascend again, to rise, to lift on high.

But, then it sails away and soars,
   and settles over the collective in prayer
      as with a falling-snow-hush in the woods.

Then it meanders and roams
   arising and falling and floating ethereally,
      gathering the vast and vibrant breath of prayer into one.

Call out, and let the Amen be yours—
   your free and unwavering reverent response,
      your loving gift,
         your every blessed breath.

Let the Amen be your bridge
   to heaven-on-earth,
      to heaven-in-your-heart,
         to God-in-your-heart,
            to God-with-you.

Let your Amen arise and be heard!
Let the Amen—sound from the depths of your soul,
and from the depths of your own Sacredness.
Let the Amen—sound on the crest of your song
and from the pulpit of your prayers.
Let the Amen—sound out in faith and in love.
So be it. Let it be so.
Amen!!!

Called

The voice in my head is clear, yet soft.
  It's present, then gone.
    So transient,
      yet so present when it's present.

The voice speaks, not in words,
  but in the nuance and nudge of wisdom,
    with the clarity and surety
      of all timeless truth.

No need for a translator,
  or an interpreter,
    for my heart and mind and soul
      comprehend the minutiae of the message.

I listen.
  In silence. In solitude.
    I await. I hope. In anticipation.
      I savor the glimpse, the glimmer,
        the showing and the shining,
          of the meaning.

It's mystical. Ethereal and airy,
  yet gratefully greening and grounding.
    It shapes my being. It directs my path.
      It fuels my inner firelight. It encourages, inspires, evokes.

I am strengthened. I am empowered. I am beckoned.

Rising on the crests of the strong,
  yet dulcet tones and soundless waveforms of my eternal essence,
    I am lifted—I wing away—I am called.

Into the Deep—I answer the Call.

More

I am *more* with God.
   I am *more* alive, and *more* energized,
      in knowing that God is with me.

I am *more* attentive, attuned, and in tune,
   with the Sacred in all of life,
      in knowing my God.

I am definitely deeper, *more* reflective, and *more* contemplative,
   in response to the subtle and the not-so-subtle nudgings,
      of God-with-me.

I am *more* hopeful, enthusiastic and optimistic,
   with God.

I am *more* content, *more* complete, and *more* whole,
   in the wonder of God's Presence.

I am *more* present,
   with God.

I am *more* ready and willing,
   with the strength I have in God.

I have a greater understanding—
   more insight—into myself, and into my community and world,
      and into humanity,
         because God is walking the journey of life with me.

I'm simply *more* of everything that is good,
   with God.

I am *more* grateful—*most* grateful—
  for all the blessings in my life—big or small—
    and I live with a heart of gratitude—
      one with God.

I am *more* with God.
  Thanks be to God.

Vignette—Theophany in the Cacophony

I had questions.
　No. I had a question.
　　A single simple burning question.
　　　Every attempt of mine
　　　　to find the right answer,
　　　　　even just the best answer,
　　　　　　failed.
　　　　　　Hopelessly failed.

I started to slip and slide, and to spiral downwards.
　My reactive anger consumed me. All of me. And I was hurting.
　　My strong, confident and brightly shining light dimmed.
　　　I desperately and restlessly
　　　　began free falling into a blackened hole,
　　　　　a deep and darkened and roily grunge pit.
　　　　　My answerless question weighed me
　　　　　　down, down, down.

I chose to go away on a solo personal retreat. There, I rested well.
　I read some evocative and inspirational books.
　　I walked multiple times in the crisp Autumn air
　　　through the nearby forest labyrinth
　　　　on the retreat property.

I chanted and sang Taize prayers in the log cabin on the shore,
　in the fresh and chilly late October evenings,
　　in the calm candlelight.

On my last retreat-evening,
　I spoke in depth with resident Spiritual Director Sister Jane.
　　She listened.
　　　She heard my heart.
　　　　She felt arising in her, the injustice in my story.
　　　　　She witnessed my angst, and my anger.
　　　　　　She saw my faith.

We shared in prayer and closed our weighted time together.
  I went to sleep, asking myself
    "What parable would Jesus tell,
      to teach the world
        how to deal with the injustice
          that I faced?"
        I fell into a
          deep deep deep
            and restful sleep.

In the morning, the final morning of my retreat,
  I leisurely lollygagged and arose quite late.
    I took my sweet time over breakfast,
      as it was pouring rain outside.
        I had planned on one more labyrinth walk
          before departing,
            but the downpour
              kept on drenching the forest.

I then chose to stall, to delay my trek to the labyrinth,
  by taking a late morning nap.
    I awoke just past the noon hour,
      to find only a gentle drizzly mist hovering in the air.

I grabbed my brolly, my Taize prayersong playlist and headset,
  and I set out for the Chartres altar.
    I entered the forest labyrinth, in silent reverent prayer.
      Not a soul was in sight
        in this deep woods Sacred space.
          I turned on my playlist
            and the choral prayersong words
              about gratitude and praise—
                these lyrics led my heart
                  into prayer.

For some forty five minutes, I walked the labyrinth path.
   My noise cancelling earphones blocked all the forest sounds,
      allowing me to sing, to chant,
         and to focus my prayerful heart.
           The umbrella over my head blocked my view
              to the overhead dome of dull grey sky.

My eyes were intentionally downcast,
   as I followed the colorful maple leaf strewn path to the altar.
      I wasn't in any hurry. I neither heard, nor saw anything,
         but my intricate pathway in the natural world.

I prayed fervently through song, through prayersong,
   in my chosen time of solitude.

And in due time, as I approached the central altar,
   I was preparing to kneel there and listen—
      listen intently—to use my hope and my trust
         and my tender faith to bring me into God's Presence.
           I had emptied myself. Humbled myself.

I was ready for God's wisdom, God's guidance,
   God's 'take' on my burning unanswered question.

Just as I began to bend my knees to kneel,
   I heard a clamorous sound beyond my choral headset sounds.
      It was a resounding cacophonous ruckus overhead,
         in the animal or bird world.
           'Squirrels squawking over spatial territory?'
           'Bird's boisterous banter?'

It was such an imperative and fervent noise,
   that I intentionally straightened up.
      I looked upward, to localize the sound.
      Slowly, slowly, I lowered my brolly.

And there before me
  was the absolute epitome of all Godly grandeur and glory!!!
  I gasped in gaping wonderment!!!

While I had been walking the labyrinth—
  with my sound-blocking-headset and my sight-blocking-brolly—
    I had not noticed that the grey clouds had all rolled back,
      revealing the magnificent forest-cathedral-view
        opening up, upward and heavenward,
          to the purest bluest skies.

The radiant sunshine was heartwarming,
  soul-warming.
    An awesome mystical, soft-filtered steamy mist
      was arising in the spacious forest realm.

There, standing at the Chartres labyrinth altar,
  with my face lifted heavenward,
    I found myself basking in the most mystical broadbeam
      of iridescently sparkling and dancing Light.
        This was truly,
          a Shimmering.
          A Shining.
            A Showing.
              A Theophany amidst the cacophony!

God's Holy Lovelight poured over me,
  through me, and into me—gracing me.
    God's Presence embraced me.
      I had literally straightened up out of the darkness,
        and into the Light.
          I felt grounded. Safe. Secure.
            I felt enlivened and energized.

But most of all, I knew that God was with me,
   and that He would walk with me through the injustice.
      When in earnest I called out—
         when Deep called to Deep—God came to me
           in a most magnificent showing
              of the Holy Lovelight,
                to remind me that I am His,
                  that I am beloved,
                    and that I will be strong,
                      in Him.

This timely gift of God's Presence is one I deeply treasure.
   I will most surely share this story again and again,
      throughout my blessed life.

This was indeed one Holy Moment.
   This was the Holy Lovelight of God gracing my darkened soul.
      This was God's Presence.
         All of the Thesaurus words in the English language
         truly fail me here.

One year later, in God's time, unannounced,
   the injustice simply went away.
      The ugliness, the villains, and the wickedness
         were all sent out packing, on pathways
           that could hurt me no more!

I didn't need to do anything!
   I didn't need to question anymore,
      or to carry my burden any longer.
         Loads lifted. Dark clouds lifted.

When I realized what was happening,
   I quickly recalled my Holy Moment
      in the deep forest altar,
         and I spoke a quiet prayer of gratitude,
            of humility, of praise to my God,
               who hears, who listens, who walks with,
                  and who is richly present to me
                     in all my earthly journeys.

Thanks be to God,
   for the Shimmering, the Shining, and the Showing—
      for the gracious gift of Presence in the Holy Lovelight.
         God is with me.
            Amen. So be it. So let it be. Amen.

Prayer Based on Psalm 42

In silence, in solitude, in prayer, I attune, I await, I listen.
  In the stillness,
    I will come to know the "Still Small Voice"[1]
      that calls out to my heart,
        that stirs up my very soul,
          that resonates and echoes
            like the sound of the Eternal
              deep in my being.

When God calls out to me,
  When "Deep calls to Deep"[2], there is a tangible sharing,
    a blessed communion,
      a wholesome interconnectedness
        a perceptible personal enrichment and abundance.

Oh God, please call on my heart.
  Let Your words, Your truth, and Your wisdom grace my being,
    that I may live out my life in loving-kindness,
      in compassion and in justice,
        that I may embody Your will in my daily living,
          that I may reach out to others,
            as You have to me,
              in love.

God, in Your depths, please call on my depths. Amen.

1. NKJV 1 Kings 19: 12
2. NRSV Ps 42: 7

CHAPTER FOUR

PSALM 46

Psalm 46 Be Still and Come to Know God

Stillness—
　The 'go to' place of refuge at the right time,
　　where the intimacy of Holy Ever-presence
　　becomes exquisitely tangible and real.

Should the earth heave, and the mountains move,
　to make monstrous tsunamis form
　　in the heart of the ocean—
　　　and should the shining waters seethe on the shores,
　　　we shall not live in fear.
　　　　Rather, we shall live
　　　　　in deep reverence and worship
　　　　　of God who strengthens us
　　　　　from the inside.

We behold our God.
　We lift God upon high, up to the heights,
　　in our worship and in our praise.

We come to stillness—
　Holy, Sacred, Savored Stillness,
　　resting in the knowledge
　　　that God provides, protects, and promises Presence,
　　　　as we reverence Him in our hearts,
　　　　　in silence, in solitude—
　　　　　　and in our time of stillness.

In our stillness,
　in the silence of our hearts,
　　we come to know our God.
　　　We are stilled in the serenity of solitude, with God.
　　　Be still and know ....[1]

1. NRSV Ps 46: 10

77

The Shape of Selah

"Selah"[1]—
    breathed out the Psalmist.

Selah—Pause,
    take a deep breath, take time.

Dwell here,
    right here, for a moment.

Just let the just-spoken-words-settle
    into your mind
        into your heart
            into your bones
                into your soul.

Hold the words,
    honor and respect the words
        and raise them up on high.

Search the words
    for the richness of their relevance
        in your daily living.

Measure the words
    and give them weight,
        and carry the words,
            in your world.

Bend the words to feel
    their flexibility
        their spaciousness
            and their place.

1. NRSV Ps 46

Tout them.
   Test them
      and try them
         for their truth.

Let the Selah enter you—
   infusing you—
      suffusing you—
         perfusing your very being.

Let the Selah surround you
   surprise you
      and serve you.

Let the Shape of Selah shape your Sacred soul. Selah

Contemplation

Contemplation, is both the intentional and incidental holding of space
for many or single fragmented thoughts, and questions,
and allowing them to float, or to take on weight,
or to dance in the Light and in the breeze,
or to filter freely through time and space,
transcending all boundaries—
perceived or real—

and then, the taking on of a sense of order, logic and priority,
and possibly emerging with more clarity and understanding,
in metaphorical, literal, lyrical and profound images
in the heart and mind.

Contemplation is an art form in itself,
rendered from the depths of the soul.
It is both appreciated and applauded
by the discerningly present 'gathered gallery'
—one's own peanut gallery
of clamoring voices!—
in one's interior being.

Contemplation, like prayer,
can bring one fully into the Presence of God,
creating a stirringly profound
Holy Moment—
a Sacred Space—
a Thin Place of the Interior Self.

Contemplation is indeed therapeutic,
and healing for the soul.
Contemplation in the stillness,
is a necessary discipline
of the mindful, mystical sage.

Contemplation courts the commonplace,
  and Contemplation courts the Light.

Contemplation is indeed, a journey—
  in the Light,
    into the Light,
      with the Light.
      Selah.

May the Light be with you, always.

Truth

Take your contemplative mind for a ride on a cloud.
A big white fluffy cloud way-way-up-up-up in the sky.
Up where currents and streams of air
flow faster than the winds down at ground level.

These powerful air masses push,
and when they pull air in from behind,
they create backflow and eddy currents
much like water filling in downstream,
behind a large-boulder-lurking in a swift-current river.
'Cloud shape-shifting' happens!

Become the cloud for a moment!
Feel the push, the pull, the drift, and the shift—
feel the desire to remain yourself, as you are,
with complete integrity and character,
and with an ambient sense
of being uniquely yourself,
steadfast and true over time.

But there are forces greater than you-the-cloud, in this universe.
Forces that illumine grounds for change,
forces that initiate first steps of evolution,
forces that incite creative and think-outside-the-box thinking
both in analytical thinking
and in problem solving—
and even in dreaming!!!

Segue for a moment. Cease to be the cloud.
And now simply sidestep in mid-air, just a little to the right or left,
and look at the cloud you were just on!
In your mind's eye, *you can do this!*

Your cloud carried you for awhile and kept you safe,
  all the while amidst a changing environment.
    It remained the same throughout, for it is still a cloud.
    But in its sameness, it still evolved.
      It faced all the forces imposed on it
        and still remained recognizable
        as a cloud.

Certain components—shape, color, size, density, moisture—
  may have emerged over time differently,
    but the cloud, is still a cloud.
      It exists in this world to do and to be as a cloud.
      The world needs clouds.

Come back now, into your contemplative mindset, down here on earth.
  Come down off your cloud, into your groundedness,
    back to your true integral self and to your inherent desire
      to know truth,
        to live truth,
          and to uphold truth
            in your ever-changing world.

Truth is a cloud.
  Over time, truth can and will change, evolve and emerge,
    as new knowledge and new understanding—and new perspectives—
    enlighten and shed light on new truths.

In the moment—
  In this moment here and now—
    truth is truth,
      and over time,
        truth, like a cloud, can shape-shift,
        truth can become,
          truth can be refreshed,
            and truth can be re-envisioned.

Our own witness of truth,
   and our own willingness to place truth at the center
    of all of our daily living,
     and our own readiness to evolve ourselves
      in the face of all imminently evolving truths—
       all of these, commit us
        to a life of integrity,
         a life of grounded living—
          and a life of grace-with-eyes-wide-open
           in our ever-evolving-way-of-being.

Feel free to look at clouds and truth from all angles,
   here and now—
    illusions and all.

Know that in this very moment,
   a cloud is a cloud.
    Know that in this very moment,
     truth is truth.

Over time, life forces can and will shape our truths,
   and, in our own grace and integrity,
    we too will be shaped by truth.

Nations need truth.
   Religious Literature needs truth.
    Social Doctrine needs truth.
     Leaders need truth—
      in Political, Religious, Educational,
       and Charismatic arenas.
        People need truth.
         Hungry minds need truth.
         Hearts need truth.
         Souls need truth.
          The world needs truth.

Truth, like a cloud, evolves.
　Truth itself, transforms.
　　Veritas lux mea.
　　　So be it. Let it be so. Amen.

Wisdom

Bigger than me.
  Greater than me.
    Deeper than me.

Elemental? Entity? Energy?
  Enlightenment versus Light itself?!
    The chicken AND the egg of the fractal equation!
    The Heavenly Horizon revealed beyond
      the mounds of Quantum Truths?!

Vast and so radically unbounded,
  yet, also a tiny tidbit—
    tangible and true.

An awesome, and most fearsome inspiration
  versus the sweet and tender intimacy
    of a personally experienced Epiphany Light.
      'AHAAAHHH!!!' versus 'ah!'

Can seemingly be knowledge, in-your-face-insistent
  as right, correct, or as a sole obvious choice,
    OR, can quietly surround-sound-you
      in a Theophany,
        in a Showing,
          in a Shining—
            even as an emanating Shimmering. Selah

Wisdom of the ages
  versus Wisdom of the moment?

Wisdom can masquerade as insight, truth and reality,
  and does so with impeccable taste and integrity.
    Sometimes.
      A masquerade is a masquerade.

Wisdom is deep.
   Resonant.
      Laced with clarity and vibrance and sheen.

Prima Facie. At first blush,
   Wisdom boldly arises out of nowhere,
      out of the depths,
         in its own planes of time and space and song.

Then again,
   if Wisdom is perpetually dwelling in the depths—
      in our own depths—
         then why is it that we find ourselves so desperate,
            in our seeking, searching,
               discerning and discovery?

If Wisdom is truly always here for our knowing,
   why do we struggle so,
      with its obtaining,
         and with its finding,
            and with its understanding?

From the Scriptures—
   "Wisdom cries out in the street, in the square she raises her voice."[1]
      Lady Wisdom, Sofia, in her mysterious nature,
         has a generous and giving, and sharing way about her.
            Not only is she Wisdom herself,
               but Wisdom is her gift that she imparts
               willingly and thoughtfully,
                  with a caring and nurturing spirit.

1. NRSV Prov 1: 20

The Wonder of Wisdom.
　The Warmth of Wisdom.
　　The Will of Wisdom.
　　　All have graced my pathways.

All have entered into my depths to find their place.
　And, all have arisen from my depths
　　as I loomed in liminal spaces,
　　　as I wrestled and reached
　　　　for new dimensions,
　　　　　boundaries and truths—
　　　　　　and as I transcended in the
　　　　　　twilight of time.

Wisdom—I call out to you.
　Wisdom—may I ever seek you, yearn for you,
　　come to know you, and cherish you—
　　　and may I ever be strengthened—
　　　　strong and sage—
　　　　　in the shimmering spell of your Light. Amen.

Spaciousness and Expansiveness

Spaciousness and expansiveness
  in our ever-active mindful energies and pursuits,
    are words that truly, feel good.
      They are both so relevant
        in describing the scope of our thinking,
          the depth of our curious queries,
            and the vastness of our present mind.

Having a wholesome spaciousness of being,
  and an ever-present expansiveness of mindset,
    allows us to enter into our profoundly contemplative realms,
      which can be likened somewhat to an eyes-wide-open 'trip',
        triggered not by psychedelics,
          rather, by our own thirsting consciousness
        and our own growing awareness.

Our inherent insatiable ghosts crave and call out,
  and disturb us into mindfulness and openness.
    Our own heightened personal degree
      of spaciousness and expansiveness,
        will lead us to increased receptivity,
          greater depths of perception,
           and, could vanquish any
            of our judgmental,
              or preconceived notions
              of the subject matter
                at hand.

Both spaciousness and expansiveness
  could be considered Spiritual Disciplines,
    in and of themselves. Selah

Spaciousness and Expansiveness
  of our whole being,
    body, mind and spirit,
      yields a time of quasi-quiescence
        and readiness and receptivity
          and mindfulness and openness—
            all good for the soul.

'Let there be an infinitely immeasurable vastness of space and time—
  360 degrees—in all three planes—in all known dimensions—
    in my approach and in my sensing—
      and in my faith in God.
        Amen!'

Metaphor and Mystery—Musings and Mumbo Jumbo

Mystery, in all of its complexity,
  and in all of its vastness,
    is a formless, faceless unknown—
      an ever-incipient realm
        of truth, façade, and dimension,
          unfolding and emerging—
            dawning in the Light.

It is smoldering in songs and in silence.
  It drives the drama in the dance of the dust.
    Present and not, its origins are
      uncomprehended, unheard of, and unseen.

It is so mystically manifest in the
  Incarnate Avatar's aura of Light!
    Its illusions are misty, wisty and wispy.
      Interestingly, inherent and integral
        in all of life itself.
          Deliciously decadent, versus
            seeming source of great dissonance,
              disharmony, discussion and debate.

Luminosity leaps and lags and lollygags
  while Mystery metaphorically meanders, mushrooms and drifts,
    curiously cloaked in a cloud of nebulosity
      which billows in, around, through and within us.

Mystery may most simply be termed
  an unanswered, or an unanswerable question.

Is there a clue?
　Is there an answer?
　　Is there a right answer?
　　　Is there more than one right answer?
　　　　Who wants the answer?
　　　　　Who's asking the question?
　　　　　　Does there need to be an answer?!
　　　　　Does the answer matter,
　　　　　　or even make a difference?!

Does the knowledge of, and the understanding of,
　Quantum Truth change the answer?
　　Or, in its deets and minutiae,
　　　does the QT presumably become the answer?!

Immaculate Conception,
　The Holy Trinity,
　　The Resurrection,
　　　The Holy Lovelight,
　　　　The Nature of God,
　　　　　The Grace of God,
　　　　　　The Presence of God—

All mysterious in nature.
　All lacking in scientific findings or support.
　　All shrouded in the Holy Mystery of the Divine.

And, isn't it just fine,
　to just let Mystery rest,
　　to let Mystery sink and settle in—
　　　and to let it find its own place?

Isn't it just free-ing and life-giving to just—
　not need to know?
　　not need to control?
　　　not need to worry or fear?

Is it not just so simple, to just—be—still—in Mystery?!

If we were to know all the answers and end all questions,
  and end all Mystery,
    God would have invited us a long time ago
      to eat from the "Tree of Knowledge"[1],
        that we might understand fully, completely and clearly,
          all of the deep and deeper mysteries.

But God did not invite us.
  We can rightfully, commonly, openly and fervently trust in Mystery.
    We can allow it to enter our very being—
      and we can welcome Mystery as it dwells within us,
        lingers with us, and sojourns with us—
          as it awakens us,
            and calls out for our attention.

We can allow Mystery to mount up in our mindfulness,
  stretching out our own spaciousness,
    etherealizing in our own expansiveness.

We can embrace Mystery with arms wide open
  and with hearts full of grace,
    resting in the knowledge
      that God is the question,
        and that God is the answer.
          God is Mystery!

Holy Mystery is very much a part of
  the Unheard, Unseen, and Uncomprehended
    God of all our hearts.

All of the metaphors in all of Creation
  can only shape, but can never define, or measure, or limit
    the Holy Mystery of God.

1. NRSV Gen 2:17

In reality and in truth,
  be still with God.
    Metaphorically speaking, be still in Mystery.
    Metaphorically be still, in Mystery. Selah

Looking Glass Wisdom

Mirror, mirror, on the wall, who's the Truest of it all?!

The Mirror doesn't lie.
   Take a good long look at what you know to be real, and true.
      Then watch the purest images
         slip from your grasp to the floor,
            shattering into millions
               of Light-reflecting pieces.

If it's truly the fate of glass to break,
   then strive with all your heart to seek the Light—the Truth—
      in all of your broken mirrors.

I stand strong, and tall.
   Shards of the broken mirror of my faith
      literally crunch and crackle underfoot,
         but they cannot cut me, or harm me,
            for I look for, and I see,
               the new Light—the new Truth,
                  in their midst.
                     And I am safe in the Light—
                       the Truth.

Look in the mirror.
   Look beyond the mirror.
      Know the mirror in its wholeness, and in its brokenness.

Always, always, always,
   remain in the Light to remain in the Truth.

A broken mirror is not the end.
   It is the beginning of new Light—new Truth. Selah

The Contemplative

We *all* have deep wells of wisdom within us.
   We Sages and Contemplatives are truly ordinary people,
      until we rise up and voice with conviction,
         the words and the images
            that stir in our hearts,
               that stir in our faith,
                  that stir in the depths of our souls.

When we step up and say something in print,
   that is unequivocally worthwhile, stirring, unique, relevant—
      and of true originality and clarity—
         we then become known for our articulations
            for our quotables
               for our logic and simple vision
                  for our depth and our insight
                     for our evocative words
                        and our very own
                           tea-rose-colored perspectives.

We *all* have something important to say.
   We *all* have something unique to share.
      We *all* have deep wells of wisdom within us.
         We *all* need to find our voice, and use it—
            to *share* the secrets of our Sage-Soul-within.
            Verba volant, scripta manent.

Stillness, Solitude, and Presence—In the Moment

Time stands still. The pace clock of life falls silent. No tick. No tock.
Time is virtually suspended.

In this chosen realm of stillness, awareness and attuning are piqued.
Distractions simply drift by, un-noticed, unacknowledged.

Heartbeats and breathing come into focus.
Gratitude simply pours into the filmy airy space—
gratitude for the wonders
of the relentless and intrepid beats and breath—
gratitude for the inherent commitment and the conviction
of beats and breath—
gratitude for life itself.

The reality of solitude wafts over the sweet scene of stillness.
It is invited. It is welcomed. It is graciously greeted
with an open heart, an open mind, and open arms.

In solitude, all earthly relational engagement and interactions cease.
Inactivity. No others. No links. No loops.
It is here, in the wideness of the moment,
in the spaciousness of time,
in the expansiveness of the spiritual,
that Sacred Presence is revealed,
known, felt, perceived—and accepted.

The moment feels Holy, Blessed,
connected to something greater than the single self—
even inter-connected
to the beat and the breath of the cosmos—
attuned to the music of the spheres.

In the stillness, in the solitude, in the moment,
   the ethereal wisp of a veil seemingly vaporizes,
      and the Holy Lovelight softly filters in,
         immersing the wholeness
            in a wash of iridescent Oneness.

Together. Bonded, yet so very free.
   In a paisley curl of unity.
      In a golden spiral of interconnectedness.
      In the finery of fractal form.
         Totally natural.
            Truly mystical, spiritual,
               wholesome, completing.

Grace. One. Unconditionally beloved as One.

Savor the Sacredness
   of stillness, solitude, and Presence, 'in the moment'.
      Our God of wisdom gave us these simple,
         yet powerful words
            "Be Still, and Know".[1]

---

1. NRSV Ps 46: 10

Breath

Breath—
    dancing in the hollow human quarters,
      in the rhythmical reality of life—
        enriching, enlivening, empowering.
          Lung 'Tidal Volumes' flow and recede,
            imperceptibly sufficing.

It keeps coming,
    until,
      it doesn't.

In, out.
    More, less.
      Quicker, lag.

A timely and sustaining gift from God.
    Exquisitely precious.
      Universally cherished.
        Greater than gold.
          Treasured jewel.
            Source of renewal.
              Befriending the energy of life.

In the best and the worst times,
    in the hardest and darkest times,
      in the sweetness of the calm after the storm—
        breathe.
          Breathe in and know, that God is with you.

Lure of Oblivion

Time loses all power, motion and form.
   Sounds muffle and mute.
      Infinity emerges, romancing the soul.

A delightfully airy, breezy state of being, settles in.
   Spaciousness of spirit and extreme expansiveness
      waltz right up to linger and frolic—
         cerebrally spontaneous, unbridled and free.

An emptying,
  a detaching,
    a disconnecting.
      A joy ride on an airborne rush,
        feet off the ground spinning and soaring,
         and arising up up up and away—
           lost, but so fancy-free-with-feet-still-on-
           the-firm-and-solid-ground.

Sent swirling and sprawling in the salty sea-spray-air,
  cast away,
    and released from the grips of the deep and the depths.

A willful freshening of spirit,
  when the brazen simplicity of the self
    leaps high and higher
      into the hallowed hollowness of all space and time.

An intentional individual choice to step out of raucous reality
  and into the full-on-carnival-dance-of-delirium,
    OR, a truly happenstance-and-chaotic-culture-
      cultivated-collectively-in-the-moment—on-a-wing-and-a-prayer!

Tuning out the noise and the pace and the rhythm of life,
and listening for the beat of the free-spirited-drummer-boy—
seeking out all of the cool and curling kaleidoscopic colors
of life lurking just beyond the craze of daily living—
releasing all commitments and cares,
likened to the large candlelit Chinese Lanterns
sent aloft on a random crescent curve
into the twilight skies.

Oblivion's tango partner is none other than
sweet moonlit reckless abandon!

Last but by no means least—the sweetly savored blissful bliss
immersing the whole body, mind and spirit,
immediately at the close of a softly spoken, fervent prayer with God—
that indescribable space of a moment,
of being overwhelmed in oblivion,
grounded in oblivion, grounded in grace—
of being held but freed—
lost but found—
lost yet held yet free—
in God's Love.

Seemingly So Selfish

Cognitive Dissonance.
    The clash that arises when knowing, saying and believing one thing,
        and then doing, or being, or living out, in the exact opposite.

It feels so very conflicted, blatantly wrong, and hypocritical,
    to live in Cognitive Dissonance.
        And I do struggle *to not be there, to not go there, and to not live there.*

I enjoy my Contemplative Life. Going Deep.
    I am experiencing the joys and the wonders
        at the reaches and at the depths of my own understanding—
            challenging myself to know and to feel more.

I feel more strongly connected to my God,
    and even more sweetly interconnected to my world,
        before, during and after my intentional contemplative sits.
            It is an exhilarating, enlightening,
                and profoundly meaningful daily practice,
                    in my own whole-person-health-and-well-being.

So, is all of my 'interior work',
    and my 'becoming more/most fully human',
    and my 'attuning to the Sacred within'—
        is all of this nothing more than a grand, self-serving,
            selfish, self-centered, wasting-of-precious-time?!

Am I truly that selfish, that I can spend a gazillion hours lost in thought,
    about matters that only concern me, and my, and mine?!

I am, only when I hold a narrow view of myself in the world.
    In only this light, indeed I am so selfish, doing all of this, for just me!
    (N.B. 90% of my prose is written in first person point of view!)

And furthermore, I have a strong negative gut reaction
  to the popular phrase 'It's all about me.'
    I find this narcissistic approach to be
      distasteful, shameful, and reproachful,
        and, I stand in judgment.
          Yet, I continue to express myself in the first person.
          Hmmmmm ....

How then, can I truthfully call myself
  a humanly considerate and compassionate soul,
    with a servant-heart, always reaching out to meet the needs
      of those in the darkness—in their darkened world—
        when I, myself, am always turning inwards,
          bettering myself, in creating 'Janis 2.0',
           becoming 'the best I can be'—
            and becoming more/most fully human??

I *am* seemingly so self-focused and 'All about me'!!
  This is my greatest personal Cognitive Dissonance!
    This is when I have to consciously stop myself, dead in my tracks.

I need to remind myself that my blessed 'interior work'
  can be and should be,
    likened to compulsory 'in-service training' in the working world.

Or, likened to my own lifelong commitment to continuing education.
  Regular and relevant, and timely in-service training—
    and continuing education
      are necessary evils in the big corporate world.

My interior work is equipping me, and shaping me,
and forming me, to do the work that I'm called to do.
I grow—my service 'to them' improves.
I learn—'they' reap.
I'm open—'they' learn by my example.
'WIN-WIN!!!'

I'm not 'Going Deep' for me!
I'm doing it to prepare for the service work
that I'm already doing in the world, for the world.
I'm listening to the call, answering the call,
and responding pro-actively to the call,
to becoming more/most fully human.
'Better me—Better world'.

When I look at this broader,
helping-myself-to-help-humanity-perspective,
I settle right down.
When I can see the real truth—the Light—I grow.
Then, I'm no longer caught up
in the pangs of Cognitive Dissonance.

Rather, I arise and lift my sails to the wind,
and I most assuredly soar onward, and upward,
in the selflessness of service to humanity.

In my stillness, I come to know the truth, myself, and my God.
Through my stillness, I selflessly serve.

Vignette—Dragonfly

The dragonfly landed on the right side of my chest,
  a few inches below my collarbone.
    I didn't dare tip my chin down to see better,
      for fear of startling it,
        and it darting quickly away in fear.

So I gazed attentively in my sharply downward sightline.
  My two friends could see the dragonfly way better than I could.
    But, *I could f-e-e-l its presence.*
      It was kind of surreal, ethereal, even mystical.
        I could feel an energy, a flow,
          a certain weighty feeling that was
            uniquely and transcendently peace-giving.

It was unusual and somewhat uncanny,
  to be so up-close-and-personal with nature.
    It made me stop in my tracks, and pay attention.
      None of us spoke for the four full minutes
        while it remained perfectly still
          on my colorful summer scarf.

The iridescent colors of the wings actually matched my scarf!
  Bronze-copper, sage green, and dusty rose hues
    sparkled vividly against the deep teal and burgundy base tones.
      This dragonfly was a stunning creature
        of pure aesthetic delight!

The interplay of Light with the iridescence of the fine fragile wings
  was compelling and exquisite.

We remained there,
  in heightened anticipation, and in appreciative wonder,
    cloaked in our shared shawl of stillness.

At about the four minute mark,
   the celestial queen lifted herself aloft
      into the warm afternoon breeze,
         and then simply vanished from our sight.

We stood there in silence,
   each of us reflecting on the wonder of the sight,
      and the meaning of the moment—
         and then each of us dwelling in, and savoring
            the ensuing seeming Sacredness.

We all felt something powerful.
   Not enchanted. Not entrancing. Not mystifying.
      Rather, we were drawn, drawn into,
         drawn deeply into, the moment.
            It was a Holy Moment.
               We felt an unexplainable Presence
                  enveloping all three of us.

Mystical and mythical lore tells us
   that when a dragonfly alights upon us and remains with us,
      our lives or our pathways will change, for the better.

This was a lovely prospect for all three of us,
   mid-week in late August,
      as we were gearing up for yet another very busy Autumn season.

But we knew in our hearts,
   that there was more than story and ancient myth drawing us in.
      We felt more.
         Our words simply fail to describe
            the extraordinary wonder,
               and the sweetness of the intimacy
                  of the moment.

We received in our hearts, all three of us,
  an overwhelming sensation of peace, and wholeness, and rightness—
  and connectedness—
    an overwhelming feeling that indeed,
    all would be well.

This was a timely and healing message for all of us,
  on our individual faith journeys and in our life journeys.
  When we recounted our thoughts and feelings
    over the weeks and months to come,
      we could not help but marvel,
        that *we all felt* that same Presence
        and same sensations,
          simply in the sighting and alighting
          of a pretty dragonfly
          in our midst.

We still to this day, cherish those few special moments
  with that magnificent dragonfly.
    It was a powerful time of attuning, and personal transcendence.
      And, true to the mysticism of the ages,
        that day became a turning point,
        a new beginning,
          a beginning of transformation,
          a time of refreshing renewal
          for all three of us.

Holy was the Moment.
  Holy is the Mystery.
    Thanks be for God's Presence in our daily living.
    Thanks be for the power of stillness
      in our faith journeys, and in our spiritual lives.
        "Be still and know!"[1]
        Vacate et scire!

---

1. NRSV Ps 46: 10

Prayer Based on Psalm 46

I am still.
   I attune to the Sacredness within me.
      I stand in awe of Your Divine Presence.
         Choirs of angels sing in my heart,
            in praise and honor of You.

I am still, and I am strong,
   in the wonder and the mystery
      of Your Name,
         of Your Essence,
            of Your Presence,
               of Your Blessedness—Your 'Blessence'!

You are my Light!
   My Rock!
      My Center!

You God, are my God, and I hold You in the highest honor.
   Sweet songs of praise spring up from my lips
      at the dawn,
         at the dark,
            and as the billion stars shine so brightly.

I am still, and in my heart of hearts,
   I know that You God, are with me. Amen.

CHAPTER FIVE

PSALM 51

Psalm 51 Seek Forgiveness

A bitter pill to swallow—
   my sin is ever before me.
    I was born guilty,
      a sinner when my mother conceived me—
       so I am told.

The Christian Church says 'born of original sin'.
   Celtic Wisdom teaches 'born of original blessing'.
    And I stand tall when I hold fast to my ancient Celtic roots.
     It's so much more comfortable
      knowing that I am born 'of blessing',
       not 'of sin'.

But, reality is here and now.
   Temptation is here, and so is the ability to take a wrong path,
    or to choose the easiest way—not necessarily the right way.
    Choosing, is part of the everyday journey.

When I know that I've chosen poorly,
   or that I've made a mistake,
    or that I could have done better,
     it is right for me to come clean,
      to seek forgiveness,
       and to get back on the right path.

It is my faith, and the wisdom of the ages,
   that are shaping my actions,
    and indeed I will be accountable.

I will maintain my integrity,
   and I will move forward with God's forgiveness,
    with God's blessing—
     with God's assurance of His love for me.

Please God, help me to know,
    and to live out the truth and the wisdom,
        that is deep deep down in my interior being.

In Your washing away of all of my falsehoods,
    and all of my falseness,
        let me arise forgiven, cleansed, and pure,
           and let me be ready to reverently attune
                to Your Presence,
                  to Your Spirit,
                    and to Your Leading—
                        with my willing spirit.
                        Amen.

Be the River—Be the Light—Be the Love

The river flows. It goes. It just goes.
  No hemming or hah-ing.
    No kicking and screaming,
      No bargaining or procrastination,
        or attaching excess negative baggage.

It just flows on, moving forward,
  around the bend,
    intrepidly over the rapids,
      shamelessly into eddy pools,
        gleefully in the waterfall over the escarpment,
          sparkling and dancing and enlivened on its journey,
        wherever that may be.

I need to embrace life.
  I need to delight exquisitely with exuberance and positive energy,
    and with trust and conviction,
      in my ever-changing, ever-moving-freshly-forward
      wonderful watercourse of life!

I need to *Be The River!*

I am born of God's Light
  and innately I carry the Holy Lovelight deep in my soul.
    It warms me, leads me, keeps me safe.
      Christ asks all of us to let our Light shine.
      Shine brightly.

There are many who walk in darkness,
  and many who have never known or experienced 'Living in the Light'.
    And many more who have yet to discover
      their very own Light within themselves.

For all of these folks, I need to embody the Christ-like Living.
I need to shine the Light for them.
I need to help them to experience
the Holy Lovelight within themselves.
I need to bring them out of their darkness
to live in the Light.

I need to *Be the Light.*

I need to *Be The Love,* and the compassion to those in need.
With my 'Celtic Eyes of the Heart,'
I need to always 'see' the needs for love and compassion,
and meet those needs by sharing my own
God-given gifts of love and compassion,
most freely,
most generously,
most unconditionally.
Genuine. Transparent.
Real—my love.

On my right path,
with a clean heart,
with God shaping my ways,
I live out my life with my personal mantra—
Be the River. Be the Light. Be the Love.
May I always be so.

Growth

Mostly imperceptible.
   Yields so much over time.
      Pregnancy and babies.
         Beautiful floral blossoms.
            More sturdy tree trunk rings.
               Impetuous pubescent forms.
                  Wisdom, insight, integrity.
                  Wrinkles and grey hair.

Simple and straightforward, or matrix of complexity.
   Pure math expressions, as in linear, compounded,
      exponential—even fractal.
      Natural, or produced, or forced.

Changing. Evolving. Developing. Transitioning.
   Perfect biology in action,
      or, proof of mathematical equations and algorithms,
         or, manifest of the magic and mystery of all life!

Sealed with the Sanctity of all living forms,
   for all life begins in Holiness—in Sacredness—
      with the Divine Presence inherent within.

An energy,
   an evolving pattern planned or random—
      a movement toward or away—
      a tangible *becoming* in the wonders of life.

Specifically Spiritual Growth.
   A dance and romance in the intangible realms,
      memorable and measureable,
         a *showing and a shining*
            in wholeness of person,
               and in balance of well-being,
               and in serenity of soul.

A touchstone of all life.

Look to the past to learn from mistakes.
   Grow into the future,
      with vision, conviction, and hope.
     Let yourself grow.
      Et crescere te.

Balanced Well-Being

Sense it. Perceive it. Feel it. Know it.
  Describe it with fresh words
    of your own understanding and experiential awareness.
    Forget the classic image of an old fashioned
      Beam Balance Scale,
        giving a market-dollar-value
          for precisely weighed goods!

When our three realms—body, mind and spirit—
  are active, functioning efficiently and comprehensively—
    creative, inspired, attuned—and virtually blossoming—
      we come to know through our personal experience,
        that sweet inner sense, of a balanced well-being.

Rest and exercise and bodily functions are natural—
  normal, timely and effortlessly at ease.
    Complications and complex challenges at work
      and along life's journey
        are met with eagerness,
          and with a willful, conquering, optimistic spirit,
          and are accomplished with a mastery
        of applied knowledge
          and fruitful brain power.

A calm-centered-positive-reverent-disciplined-hopeful-
  forgiven-and-forgiving-loved-and-loving-approach,
    completes the picture of a balanced
    and wholesome well-being.

May each of your days, your hours, your moments,
  arise on the crest of well-being,
    and ride onward, forward,
      with a certain confidence and grace,
        that you may aspire, know, feel,
          see, be, and become
            that pristine image
              of beautiful, blessed,
                blissful balance,
                  in body, mind, and spirit.

May you experience the Trinity of Wholeness—
  in body, mind, and spirit.

Dreams

No details.
  No boundaries.
    No sense of time.
      No direction.
        No clear pathways or connections.

Only—
  Cloudiness of clarity!
    Reflections of reality.
      Iridescence of inspiration.
        Eloquence of evil.
          Flamboyance of fear.
            Darkness of desperation.
              Nuance of nothingness.

Curl of conscience.
  Whiff of wisdom.
    Suggestion of the sagacious.
      Mirage of mystery.
        Magic in the moment.
          Muse of the mystic.
            Mirror of mindfulness.
              Seeming senescence.

Evocative energy.
  Erupting of the eros.
    Bangin' jangin' bliss.
      Rising of the river.
        Shape-shifter of the soul.

Sail on.
  River on.
    Arise upon—
      the mountain, the message and the meaning,
       of your articulate dreamscapes rising—
        in your luminescence,
         in your depths,
          in the very Light of your being.

Clean Heart, Right Spirit, Willing Spirit

In a world of free will,
   wrongs, wrong-doings, and wrongfulness reside.
    Big or small, giganormous or infinitesimal,
     wrong is wrong, and can be made right.

I come to God aware of my will, my ways, and my wrongs.
   I come in prayer to make things right.
    I come with a contrite heart.
     I humbly vow
      to do better,
       to be better,
        to better myself and my ways.

And God of my heart
  receives me
   welcomes me,
    and blesses me.

God, in all of His righteousness and in His judgment,
  knows my heart, knows my soul, and knows me,
   and offers His forgiveness,
    and His assurance of pardon,
     and His unconditional love.

God in His own way
  "creates in me—
   a clean heart,
    a right spirit,
     and sustains me with a willing spirit"[1].

And, my grateful heart bows
  in gratitude and reverence—
   and in praise.
    Thanks be to God, Amen.

1. paraphrase of NRSV Ps 51: 10

Fresh Start

I was busted, and broken.
  I owned up and confessed.
    And You made me whole.
      I stood and emptied myself at Your feet.
        You immersed me
          in the great well of forgiveness.
            My sin and transgression
              became ripples of bygones.

My slate is now clean.
  Now I move forward with Your help, God,
    in a fresh start
      with a clean heart[1],
        given by You,
          gifted by You.

Please let me know Your Presence,
  and let me sense the movement of Your Spirit
    in all my ways,
      in all my days.

Let my repentant heart become my altar,
  my right path,
    the Thin Place of my interior being.
      Amen.

1. paraphrase of NRSV Ps 51: 10

Vignette—Time to Forgive

We were seated side by side, in the very centre of a long couch,
  in front of a crackling fire in the fireplace,
    on a cold Canadian February afternoon,
      at the nursing home.

She, in her elder years,
  was shrinking in her physical stature,
    and sadly, in her cognition.
      In the throes of Alzheimer's Disease,
        she did indeed know me,
          and she would call me by my name,
            but, she really had no memories
              or actual recall of the past.

It felt very right for me, in the moment,
  to put my arm around her frail shoulders,
    and to gently draw her in closer to me, to my side.
      As she leaned her body,
        and inclined her head onto my chest,
          she spoke softly
            "This is nice. Really, really nice."

My mind was suddenly racing, and working at break-neck speed,
  as memories of our ugly past
    burst through the dams of conscious repression,
      and they gushed into my here and now.

Mom and I historically, were like oil and water.
  We differed greatly
    in opinion, and in approach, and in perspective.
      Our personalities clashed,
        and often a contest of wills
          would cut off our communication,
            and keep us wary, distanced, and apart.

Indeed, some harsh words were spoken, over the years.
　Unfortunately some words can never be un-said,
　　and they had the power to hurt, and scar, and cripple—and poison.

As our tender moment unfolded there on the couch,
　my own personal epiphany shone brighter
　　than the sparkling fire before us.

I said to myself
　"Why on earth am I holding onto—
　　and harboring all of the angst of the past,
　　　and still carrying the burden of hurt and guilt and shame?
　　　　I'm always seething with my unforgiveness.

It's so blatantly obvious that mom has no recall
　of any of our clashes and harsh words.
　　In her dementia, she is oblivious.
　　　She is free of the grievous tensions between us".

I turned my heart to God in prayer
　"Dear God, please forgive my mom, and forgive me too.
　　Our old ways seem to be behind us now.

Please take my falseness and take my falsehoods,
　and shape mine into a clean and vibrant and wholesome heart.
　　Please guide me, God, into Your will and Your way,
　　　through the wonders of Your Spirit."

I paused and collected my words.
  "And please God, bind us together
    in the warmth of Your love,
      and let us live out our earthly days
        in Your peace,
          in Your grace,
            and in Your love.
              Hold us, embrace us, keep us.
                Amen."

A hollow silence tingled in our midst.
  We were alone by the fireplace,
    but indeed, we were not alone, for God was with us.
      My loads and cares and burdens
        were now all willingly cast into space,
          nevermore to weigh me down again.

It wasn't long before Mom had two successive bouts of pneumonia,
  in March and in May,
    and after a short five-day bedside and overnight vigil,
      she passed out of this earthly place
        and into the realm of Eternal Light and Love.

Our lifelong testy relationship had been healed,
  through the wonders of my simple fireside epiphany,
    and my contrite heart.

My forgiving heart brought me
  a welcomed peace
    and a richness of contentment
      that I should have known many many many years ago,
        had I forgiven,
          and sought forgiveness sooner.

I walk taller now,
   and breathe easier now,
      in not carrying around the fires of my unforgiveness
      in my daily living.

I've moved on with my clean heart,
   and with my willing spirit,
      knowing a better quality of life
         through the act of forgiving
            both my mom and myself.

How cathartic.
   How freeing. How contented I am now—
      Thanks be to God.

Prayer Based on Psalm 51

Dear God,
   It is written "Create in me a clean heart,
      and put a new and right spirit within me."[1]

I am not perfect.
   I have wandered and strayed.
      I have floundered.
         In my stubbornness and in my arrogance,
            and in my spiteful contempt,
               I have dug my heels down hard and deep.

I have searched and questioned and contested.
   And, in the grace of Your forgiveness,
      You send me forward, cleansed, fresh,
         and strengthened by Your Spirit.

I know that with You, and through You,
   I will always move forward in the Light, back on track—
      empowered in Your love and mercy.

I come to You, with my broken and contrite heart.
   You enter my heart and Your forgiving power leads me onward.
      And, I manage to find my way.
         Thanks, Thanks, Thanks be to You, Oh God.

1. NRSV Ps 51: 10

CHAPTER SIX

PSALM 55

Psalm 55 Rest Safely with God

Please turn to me, Oh God,
    and listen fiercely, to hear my earnest voice in prayer.

Oh, that I had wings like a dove!
    I would fly far away and be at rest![1]
        Oh, to lodge in the wilderness.
            Oh, build me a nest in the wilderness.
            I would have shelter.
            I would be safe.

In the calm of the wilderness,
    in the stillness of the Holy Lovelight,
        I would just rest,
        I would just be,
            I would find You.

Oh, for the wings of a dove!
    Oh God of grace, Oh God of my heart
        Hear my prayer. Hear my heart.
            So be it. So let it be. Let it be so. Amen.

1. NRSV Ps 55; 6

Real. True. And Sure—As Sure as the Sun Rises

Beyond the cloud is sunshine.
    Above the curl the wave-crest.
        Beneath bird-wings are feathers—
            Real. True. And sure—
                As sure as the sun rises.[1]

Behind the tide is moon-power.
    Around the sage is wisdom.
        Beside still waters the calm—
            Real. True. And sure—
                As sure as the sun rises.

Within my soul the River.
    Deep in my heart the Shinings.
        Born of the Holy Lovelight—
            Real. True. And sure—
                As sure as the sun rises.

I am safe.
    I am secure.
        I am strong—
            Real. True. And sure—
                As sure as the sun rises.

1. TNIV Hos 6:3

Sanctuary Me

Render me
  silent, calm, free,
    at rest indeed,
      "beside the blessed, clear and deep
      still still waters."[1]

Let me draw my life-giving breath
  in the Light, in the love,
    in the peace, in Your grace—
      in the depths of my soul-surrendered faith.

Attune my whole being to all that is Sacred,
  Shimmering, Shining, Aligning,
    and usher my own tender Light into Your Presence,
      into the Lovelight—Your Holy Lovelight, God.

May the union of our Light
  become an aura, a beacon,
    a lighthouse in the night,
      a safe haven, quiet haven—
        a welcome Sanctuary for those who journey without Light.

May my body, mind and spirit
  breathe, delight, alight,
    as I slowly segue, simmer, and shine
      in this Sanctuary of our Light.

Please God,
  Hold me.
    Harbor me—
      Sanctuary me.
        Amen.

1. paraphrase of NRSV Ps 23:2

Lost, Yet Held—Lost in Wonder, Mystery and Grace

Here I stand. Here I am
   in a place of my own choosing
      spending time in my own doing.

Time rests
  in life's best
    just need to get
      off the wheel—
        the *Original Sin Spinning Wheel*—
          and lose my falsely fervent zeal.

I need to float—be free—
  and soar—find me.
    I need to take wing and sing
      I need to *Stop*—
        and—be—still.

I'll fly beyond the shore where I can see.
  I'll fly beyond the heights where I can feel.
    I'll fly—on by—and sigh—
      Goodbye to the old me!

For my heart is undergoing.
  My faith is ever-growing.
    My Holy Ground just shook.
      It's rockin' and a rollin'—
        With fresh new eyes I read The Book!

What grounded me has set me free.
  What *held me,* back then
    now sets me right, on track again.

Rebirthing. Re-turning. Discerning.
Transforming. Transcending.
    Alive and alert. Awake, attuned, aware—

I care! And I dare
    to dream—to dream big
        to get lost—so lost
            to seek—mystery
                to hold—mystically
                    to see—with clarity
                        to see so much more
                            than I did before!

For now I see with my heart,
    and every day is a mighty fine start!

My heart has eyes!
    I realize—I recognize—
        The Holiness, The Sacredness, The Blessedness,
            of every living thing,
                of every living soul,
                    of every time and every space,
                        of every Godly-given grace—
                            in all created things!!!

One with God, God with me.
    Born of goodness, born of Light.
        Born of God's Holy Lovelight.

Beloved.
    Befriended and Befriending.
        Being.
            Becoming wholly me!

Here I stand
  interconnected with all that is—
    breathing, thriving, yearning, learning,
      in the midst, yet beyond,
        at the center, at the edge,
          in the calm and in the storm,
            in what seems to be new,
              but, in what is deeply rooted
                in the ancient—
                  in the Eternal.

Lost in wonder, mystery and grace.
  Lost—in a good way!—in God.
    Totally *lost* in all that matters most.

Lost, yet, *held*—
  Held fast in my faith—
    Held firm in my chosen paths—
      Held safely in my wholeness.

Held securely in the Light.
  Held warmly and tenderly, in the Love.
    Held, by God.
      Amen.

There Is No Darkness

All is not dark—
For even in the darkness, there is Light.

Mystery is not dark.
  The unknown is not dark.
    Even the intangible and unimaginable are not dark—
    for even in the darkness, there is Light.

Winters may be long and bleak.
  Health may be frail and declining.
    Finances may seem dark and gloomy
    and overwhelming—
      but—even in the darkness, there is Light.

The ancient and unprecedented
  unknown journey on the ark
    led to a magnificent rainbow.
      The first rainbow ever!

The Israelites wandering in the desert
  led the way to building strong and powerful
    nations and religions.

The motley crew of disciples of Jesus
  who answered the call "Come Follow Me!"[1]
    became the leaders of the early Christian Church.

These journeys, wanderings and followings
  were all likely uncertain, uncomfortable, scary—
    even at times, dark.

But, they all moved forward—
  resting in the knowledge that even in the dark, there is Light.

1. NRSV Matt 4: 19

Jesus is the Light of the World.
  Nothing is impossible in Him
    who bears the Light of the World.
      Nothing is impossible in Him.
        Nothing is impossible.
          Nothing nothing nothing is impossible!

Let us lift our faces to the Light.
  Let us open our minds to the paths of Light before us.
    Let us reach out with hearts and hands
      to the Light that has promised
        to lead us through any darkness.

Let us welcome and embrace the Light.
  And then, *let us be the Light!*—in our community and in our world.

Let us shine brightly for all to see.
  Shine brightly, so that no one knows the darkness—
    so that no one fears the darkness.

There is no darkness, only Light.
  Non est nisi lux tenebris. Amen.

I Am Safe. I Am Strong. I Am More.

In sailing on the stormy seas
  or settling on the shore
    beside the sparkling waters still,
      I'm safe. I'm strong. I'm more.

I am *safe*—
  resting on the Holy and experiential doctrine of God-with-me.
    In this secure harbor and haven,
      my doubts and my fears, and all of my unknowns,
        drift away in the currents
          as I stand tall on land or sea,
            trusting in my God's ever-presence with me.

I am *strong*—
  always, for God is with me, always.
    On the bow of my boat, my heart takes on a banner
      of courage, strength, and will,
        cresting all the waves, riding on the knowledge
          of God's Eternal Presence within me.

I am *more*—
  with God-who-is-more.
    I am planing, and surging forward
      with wisdom, with comfort, and with confidence—
        I am more—
          in knowing
            that I am born of the Light of God,
              born of Original Blessing,
                born of Essential Goodness—

And, I am more—
in believing
that the Holy Lovelight dwells in me,
lighting me and leading me,
holding me in Holiness and Love,
in all my journeying days.

Safe. Strong. More. Me!
Thanks be to God.

Vignette—Beaver Dam

We were not lost. Yet.
    It was late afternoon of day-five,
        on a seven-day wilderness canoe trip
            in Temagami, Ontario, Canada.

Sun would soon set at 630 PM.
    Pristine waterways, favorable sunny weather,
        cool-ish September nights
            with NO mosquitoes by the evening campfire,
                rugged and challenging portages overland between lakes—
                all made for a great outdoor adventure
                    in the remoteness of God's Country!

Rarely would we see another soul
    out on the waterways or on the trails.
        We were together, yet alone,
            way way out there.

We were portaging on a half-mile route alongside a shallow river,
    when suddenly our portage trail simply vanished underfoot.
        It completely disappeared from our sight.
            It was soon very evident that the beavers
                had successfully dammed up the river nearby,
                    causing extensive flooding above their dam site.
                        The flood waters had spread over the trail,
                            making it impossible to visualize
                            'the way' through the forest.

What to do?! We couldn't go back—
    Families expected us in two days' time.
        To go back was five days.
            They would worry if we were that late,
                and they would send search parties out for sure!
                    Going back was not an option!

I prayed out loud "Oh, for the wings of a dove,[1]
  that we might soar above the floodwaters in the wilderness,
  and find the trail—the path to lead us home, to rest."

As we were mulling over our options,
  acutely aware of our impending loss of daylight,
    we heard a noisy commotion and some voices in the woods.
    Coming through on the trail from the opposite direction
      was another portaging group!

They were standing on the dry trail!
  We could then see precisely where to go, to get through on
    the flooded mucky unmarked forest trail!
    We had a 'wee hoot and holler'—
      an emotional eruption in joyful laughter.
      We were relieved—and safe!

They saw us, and they were just as relieved to see us, as we them!
  We headed straight for each other,
    through the soggy-boggy-sink-to-your-knees-
    newly-dammed-up-forest-floor,
      and then we continued on beyond them, to the dry trail.

We never would have found our way through,
  without first sighting them on the trail just beyond the flood zone
  at that very moment!

They appeared to us in our time of need,
  much like angels appear when they are needed.
    I know that God keeps us safe, and leads us,
      in sometimes baffling and mysterious ways.
        God kept us and the other portagers safe,
          at the right time, in His time—
            thanks be to God
              who showed us the way.

1. NRSV Ps 55: 6

The rest of the trip was beautiful, and thankfully uneventful, and we were home on time, in two more days, as planned.

Yessss!

God is good!!!

Prayer Based on Psalm 55

Dear God,
   I fly.
      I wing my way through life
         yearning to find You,
            seeking to lodge with You,
               longing to rest with You.

And this brings me joy, comfort, solace and hope.

May my wings ever lead me to You.
   May I never lose my inborn need for You,
      and, may I always find You,
         wherever in the wilderness I come to rest,
         wherever in the wilderness I build my nest.
         Wherever in the wilderness,
            I will feel blessed, by You.
            Amen.

CHAPTER SEVEN

PSALM 63

Psalm 63 Seek God's Presence and Provision

I have thirsted and found water.
   I have fallen down flat with fatigue, and found rest.
     I have been sheltered, been given sanctuary,
       and I've found strength on my journey.

Prayerful words come to my lips,
   as the sun and moon
     court in the twilight sky.
      I sing my songs of joy,
        as my heart soars
          on wings of gratitude.

I am beloved, chosen, called,
   and from this cradle of comfort,
     I rise up—
       sure in my faith,
        savvy in my knowing,
         solid in my conviction,
          for the veil is thin,
           and I stand on the right,
          in Your Presence,
         in the moment,
          in the Light.

Essence

God's Holy Lovelight
  is the very essence
    of the Sacred in me—
      of my body, mind and spirit—
        of my very being—
          of my soul.

With the Lovelight,
  the spaciousness of my heart
    and of my consciousness
      and of my interconnectedness
        knows no boundaries.
          I am alive.
            I am open.
              I am real,
                with the Light.

Through the Lovelight,
  a creative energy arises up in me, surging swelling soaring stirring,
    to offer up
      the shape, the form, the poetry,
        the cadence and rhythm of the music and dance
          and the colour/texture/depth
            of my quickening artistic creations.
              Creativity is kindled, born,
                and enlivened in me,
                  through the Light.

In the Lovelight,
    I am safe, strong, secure, and centered.
        I am faithfully formed and spiritually formed.
            I am basking in the Light
                through all the mysteries of life
                    as God's Beloved.
                        I am truly, unconditionally loved,
                            in the Light.

God's Holy Lovelight
    is the very essence of the Sacred—
        of the Sacred-in-me.
            Selah

What Does Matter

It doesn't matter—
　　the Name you use
　　　　to call out to God.

It doesn't matter—
　　how you know
　　　　or how you see
　　　　　　your God.

It doesn't matter—
　　the vocabulary you use
　　　　to describe the Presence of God.

What does matter—
　　is that you have an open and reverent,
　　　　and faithful relationship with God,
　　　　　　and that you receive strength and comfort
　　　　　　　　in knowing your God.

What does matter—
　　is that in your own seeking of God,
　　　　God is seeking you.

What does matter—
　　is your presence seeking God's Presence.
　　Presence seeking Presence.

Contentment

Contentment—

A place of being whole.
  A calm and carefree mindset, heartset, and soulset.
    A realm where all needs are met,
      wants are non-important, even non-existent,
      and colorful dreams abound.

A sense of balanced well-being
  of body, mind and spirit.

A generative state where creativity, ingenuity, and inspiration flow,
  blurring boundaries,
    and surging on with primal and reckless abandon.

A time of complete connectedness,
  and the comfort of interconnectedness,
    yet still, a growing and dynamic sense
      of freedom, spaciousness, and expansiveness.

A sense of loads lifted,
  and clouds lifted—
    leaving a welcomed weightlessness,
      and a breezy buoyant bliss.

An overwhelming sense of rightness, and goodness, and wellness.
  An intuitive sensibility of 'being-at-home'—
    in a wholesome, havenly home—
      in the mystical, spiritual, and ethereal worlds.

Being grounded and sure,
  yet metaphorically dancing through life
    with no feet on the ground,
      with an uplifting awesome airy aura,
        and a phenomenal freeing of spirit.

Being simply, or even abundantly, fulfilled.
  Being complete.
    Being blessed.
      Being whole.
        Being One.

Contentment—
  so wanted, desired, dreamt of, prayed for, sought.

Contentment—
  the new middle-name
    of my contemplative soul.

In You, oh God,
  I thirst no more.
    I am content.
      Amen.

Showings, Shinings and Shimmerings

Showings, Shinings, and Shimmerings,
   are the Lovelight expressions of God.
      Life-giving. Life-changing. Life-blessing.

Not at all virtual,
   rather, wholly and tangibly real.
      Larger-than-life-present-here-and-now.
      The grandeur-of-God-here-and-now.
      The Presence-of-God-here-and-now.

I am indeed blessed—
   ever-blessed,
      and showered
         in the Light—
            The Holy Lovelight of God.

God's Light is as water
   to the parched.
      I thirst no more.

Breeze and Wind—Presence

Breeze—

A fresh and gentle brushing, or breath, of wind.
  Intimately present—can touch and caress, and excite.
    Nuance of the ethereal.
      Nudge of the spiritual.
        Norm of the weather and Mother Nature!

Cooling, refreshing—
  or chilling, recoiling.

Featherweight friendly reminder
  of Your ever-presence.

How does something so invisible
  infuse and inspire us so deeply?!

How does the almost imperceptible
  permeate our depths?!

How fair,
  and how fine the moment—
    the breeze
      through the trees
        while I'm on my knees
         with You!

Wind—

On the move.
  Fairer skies or foul weather coming—
    wind seems to move the weather along.

Wind as a herald.
  Wind as a tell.
    Wind as a foretelling of things to come.

Powerful, intrepid, relentless, and scathing,
  versus peaceful, precious, life-supporting, and pure.

Never ever inert.
  Never ever alone.
    Always part of something greater.
      Ever evocative, good or bad.
        Ever-stirring, rustling, whispering.

Worthy of my wonder, wit, and whimsy.
  Transcending time and space, and eternity—
    Wind—my mysterious mystical muse.

Breeze and Wind—
  Poetic. Present. Presence.
    Selah

God's Perfect Peace

I reach instinctively for his hand,
    as we stroll along barefoot on the sandy shores, at sunset.
        His deeply crevassed hand is warm and oversized, cradling mine.
        I feel secure. Safe. Contented. Sure.

Our feet make side-by-side-parallel tracks
    of casually ambling imprints in the sand,
        much like those in the famous poem.
          Over my shoulder I gaze back upon them and smile.
        I linger in the joy of the moment,
          right here, right now.

Timid lackadaisical shoreline waves advance and recede, and in time,
    they erase the footprinted evidence
        of our sunset stroll on the sandy shores.
        'No trace'.

I realize that although our footprints have vanished from sight,
    that they are still very real.
        They, in their absence, now symbolically represent
          the moments of our journey together, here and now,
            and our seeming interconnectedness and Oneness.
          Such a powerful symbol to cherish.

The evening breeze is silky soft, gentle, quiet.
    It comes from away, from across the bay,
        from the beaches and the reaches
        of the far western shore, and more.

Occasional wee puff patterns
    sweep over the deep—
        over the calm waters—
          not an evening
            for sailboats for sure!

The finest nuance of the sweet breath of wind reminds me
that I am part of something much greater than my single self,
and that indeed all life is interconnected
in both seen and unseen ways.
I feel arising in me an earthy groundedness—
a wholesome Oneness—
and a heartfelt trust
that all is well
here in this moment,
and in this space,
and within me.

We stop walking, just because.
And we turn our faces to see the great orange fireball
floating—hovering—sinking—
and being swallowed up whole, into the horizon.
Together, we step forward
into the cool, ankle deep shallows.

No words are spoken.
Our hands are still linked, palm to palm, fingers interlaced,
as we stand in silence,
lulled by the lightly lapping sounds
of the refreshing waters over our feet.

I lean to my left, onto his right shoulder.
With my head inclined,
the horizon is now off-kilter in my eyes.
But, I stand steady and strong, and serene,
in this tender Lovelit moment.

He releases my hand to hold me around my waist.
  His embrace is so symbolic of our unspoken emotions.
    We both sense
      that we are being held, embraced,
        enfolded-in-and-by the fading sunset light.
          There is a novel nuance—
            a mystical nudge.
              Perhaps a Holy Moment
                is unfolding in our midst?!

Here, in the grandeur of God's Holy Lovelight,
  in our wide-open-receptivity,
    we instinctively choose to attune to the Sacredness—
      to the Presence—
        to God's Perfect Peace.

In our shared silence,
  God, in His own strong yet subtle way,
    is making His Presence known to both of us.

The Holy Lovelight iridesces and dances over the waters,
  calling us deeper into the mystery of the milieu.
    In our humility, in our open-ness and grace,
      we surrender to the wonder,
        and allow ourselves the momentary privilege
        and the freedom of just being—
          of just being in the present—
          of just being in the Presence—
            of just living and breathing in the now—
              in the Perfect Peace of God.

Words fail here.
  Perfect Peace cannot be defined by words,
    rather, it must be experienced,
      encountered, savored, breathed, lived,
        and taken in, wholly and completely.

God's Perfect Peace must be literally soaked in.
　　Immersion is close.
　　　Bathed in, or washed over by,
　　　　or flowed upon, or poured over.
　　　　Intimately gathered in close.
　　　　Suffused, infused,
　　　　　permeated, infiltrated.
　　　　Drawn into.
　　　　Selah

Find yourself some time.
　　Find your own mystical or spiritual realm, or centering place.
　　　Commune there in solitude.
　　　　Take time and attune yourself to the Sacred in your midst.
　　　　And just be.

God's Presence can and will be sensed,
　　felt, experienced and savored.
　　　"God's Perfect Peace passes all understanding"[1],
　　　　but it is yours for the having,
　　　　　yours for the receiving,
　　　　　　yours, for just simply being
　　　　　　a humble child of God.

May God's Holy Lovelight shine on you,
　　shine into you,
　　　and shine through you,
　　　　bringing you into God's Perfect Peace.

Peace be with you, my friend, now and always.
　　Peace—blissful, and heart-overflowing-purest peace.
　　　Holy-and-Blessed-deep-deep-peace to you, my friend.
　　　Amen.

1. NRSV Phil 4: 7

Janis versus Jacob—I Will Wrestle Not

"Jacob wrestled with God. In a dream. And he lived to tell the story.
Peniel was the place of Jacob's meeting, face-to-face-with-God."[1]

+++

I feel conflicted. I live the Contemplative Life.
  I am always actively seeking and searching.
    Yet, despite all of my constant questing and questioning,
      I am deeply contented and serene.
        I am not restless, rather, *I am* wholly at peace.

I delight in attuning intently
  to the Sacred in my midst,
    to the Sacred within.
      I open myself freely, frequently, fully, to God.
      And this serves me well.

I live, like Jacob, seeking out my own 'Peniel',
  where I too, can come into the Presence of God.
    I dwell in the perpetual hope
      that I might still one day, *see my God, face-to-face!*

I pray for faith, not fear, in those precious Holy Moments.
  I pray for grace, face-to-face,
    to bow, to be on bended knee,
      to breathe—to just be—with God.

I pray that peace and contentment and gratitude
  will ever roll, like resounding echoes,
    in my songs and in my prayers—
      in my heart, and in my whole being—
        in God's Holy Presence.

1. Paraphrase of NRSV Genesis 32: 22–30

I pray for innermost strength in my personal Peniel.
In all of my contemplative sits, *I will find contentment.*
By the grace of God, *I will rest in God's peace—*
I'll simply *be with God—*
I will wrestle not!—
I will wrestle not!
Selah

Healing

To heal,
  is not to cure.
    Rather, to heal is to bring
      the wounded, the unwell, and the weary,
        to a-place-of-acceptance-of-their-journey—
         to a-place-of-contentment-of-the-heart—
          to a-place-of-perfect-peace—
        despite all that ails them,
         or brings them harm.

To heal, is to bring God
  into their daily rhythm,
    into their consciousness,
    into their awareness,
    into their heart—
      that God's Presence alone
        will bring comfort and care,
         equipping them with hope
          for their healing journey.

God's welcomed ever-presence—
  is the very heart of healing—
    the blessed gift of healing that only God can bring.

The Healing

He was bent, twisted, emaciated in his bed.
  His heart beat to the rhythm of loneliness and despair.
  I spoke his name—he could not answer.
  His eyes were open—staring.

I covered his shoulders with his afghan.
  I raised the blind to bring in the Light.
  I spoke of daisies in meadows,
    and songbirds of joy—mirth!
    And feathers in Lovelight—
      floating gently to earth.

I spoke of the morning—my morning.
  I spoke of my dreams—my tomorrows.
  I spoke of—my heart.

He turned his staring gaze toward me.
  He looked deeply into my soul.
    His eyes spoke his story.
    His eyes spoke his pain.

And then,
  His eyes spoke his gratitude.
  His eyes softened as they spoke to me.

He reached out to touch my arm.

For a weighted moment
  we shared in each other's humanity.
    Our hearts connected.
      We became fast friends of the heart.
      We were healed.
        Indeed we were healed.

We were—
    silent, sensing,
        sharing, supporting, savoring.

We were—
    attuning, knowing,
    understanding—
        we were loved and cared for.

In the Presence of God,
    in the warmth of Holy Lovelight,
      with hearts wide open,
        with God's grace pouring out—
        Grace healed us.
          Compassion bonded us.
        Love grounded us.
          God was with us—
            Thanks be to God.

Dark Nights in the Depths

Tragedy struck last week.
  Life was lost right before us.
    A beloved gift of precious life that had enriched all of our lives,
      lived no more.
        A fragile little life was snuffed out—wrenched away—
          mired in mystery—dark, dark mystery.
            Shroud. Cloud. Grief. No relief.

Then "Why?" and "How come?"
  and the bargaining "What if?" and "If only."

Fear. Anger. More answerless questions. Hopelessness.
  Despair tumbled and teamed up with guilt and shame.
    It all needlessly piled up higher and deeper—
      drenching and chilling,
        and weighing us down, down, down.

Paralyzing woe tore into our hearts.
  Adrift we were, in the sea of emptiness,
    of vastness and immensity—
      devoid of hope—
        barren, bereft, without. *Sans.*
          Lost.

I knew in my heart that God was with us,
  but I just couldn't call out to Him.
    I just couldn't feel Him. And, I didn't even try to find Him.

I crawled into the dark nights of my own dismal depths—
  and there, sorrow arrested my faith.
    Shaken and shivering, I let darkness overcome my Light.
      I was stuck there, in a living, breathing Hell.

Time moaned and groaned, labored and lagged.
  Nights went on and on, forever.
    Tick tarried, and lost its friend—tock.
      Sleep didn't come.
        Dark circles, apathy, and cranky pants
          sheltered in place with me.

And soon, I sorely needed comfort.
  I so needed the warmth of the Light—God's Light.
    I needed to venture out of the hole, the pit, the darkness,
      and to stand up tall in the Light.
        I needed to open myself to the Light—
          the Light that I've always believed
            was ever-with-me.

I desperately needed God's all-embracing-Light—
  like a wrap-around-hug-of-strength-and-hope.
    So, I chose to open up—
      to open my very being.

Symbolically I stretched both of my hands upward, outward—
  toward the Light.
    In complete humility and petition,
      my fragile darkened soul reached out to the Light.

And truth be told, the Light was there. I felt it. I wanted it. I needed it.
  Shining. Shimmering—
    there to bath my wretched brokenness—
    there to lift up all of my lost-ness—
      there to bind my wounded heart—
        there to lighten my heavy and hurting soul.
          My healing could begin. I was ready.

And as time sallies forth,
my continued self-opening is being rewarded.
I am stronger.
My faith faltered for sure,
but, it will never, ever fail me.
And—lesson re-learned—
I just need to look for the Light—
always, always, always,
look for the Light.

In the dark, in the depths, the Light *is* ever-shining.
I know this. I now need the grace and the grit
to embody this—to live this—
in all of the turbulence and in all of the throes
of seeming tsunamic, or tornadic tragic loss.
Thanks be to God who lights my world.
Amen.

Vignette—Moonbeam

The road was long.
   The journey was over.
      I was coming home unfulfilled, lost, and broken.
      I carried a hollow empty hurting
         that no one could really understand.
            I had no energy to even yearn.
               My heart was heavy,
                  and hope was nowhere to be found.

My first night home, I could not sleep.
   The void in my heart was overwhelming me,
      and stirring up a storm of restlessness
         like I'd never known before.

I got up to walk around,
   and 'something' made me go to the big bay window.
      My life was about to change.
         I was about to receive the most precious Godly gift—
            that which surpasses all human understanding.

Above me in the twinkling midnight sky,
   was the quintessential silvery moon.
      Its glimmering, shimmering moonbeams
         were in that very moment—incredibly bright.
            They were expansive pyramid-like showings
               of sparkling colored lights.

Where the moonlight met the sloping snowy surface of our front lawn,
   snow crystals danced and iridesced
      with sheer abandon and delight.

The mystical Light
　reached right through the grand floor-to-ceiling window.
　It encircled and embraced my whole being.
　　I couldn't move!
　　　I had the strangest sensation of being filled—
　　　　of being filled slowly, but surely—
　　　　　of being nurtured and cared for,
　　　　　　and held—
　　　　　　　embraced by the Light.

An all-encompassing peace washed over me.
　Peace filled me.
　　Peace healed my brokenness and my emptiness.
　　　Peace steered me into the wholesome realm of contentment.
　　　　Then, peace pointed perfectly to hope.
　　　　　And hope filled me too.
　　　　　　My spirit lifted
　　　　　　　and my soul was no longer sinking,
　　　　　　　　bereft or broken.

And I knew then, that God was present to me, yet again,
　in His Holy Lovelight.
　　God graced me with Holy Presence,
　　　and graced me with His Holy Lovelight.

From that moment forward, I knew what it meant,
　to know the peace of God,
　　"the peace that passes all understanding."[1]
　　　'Message in a moonbeam',
　　　　'Presence in peacefulness',
　　　　　'Hope for the humble',
　　　　　　'Safe. At rest. Perfect, perfect peace.'

1. NRSV Phil 4: 7

God works in such mysterious ways.
  God *could not* change the source of my emptiness,
    but He *could* be present to me,
      and equip me for life's journey.
        God gifted me with His peace.
          Both God's Presence and God's Provision—
            given to me,
              in one perfect gift of moonlit peace.

And I move forward in life
  knowing that God is present to me, with me,
    in the darkness and in the Light.
      I live securely now in this truth,
        and I will hold this truth deep in my heart,
          through all my days.

Prayer Based on Psalm 63

Dear God, I have thirsted for You
   in the dry deserts of the world.
      I have worshipped and prayed
         and sung out praises to You.

And You have come to me,
   and taken me into Your wing,
      and You have set me apart, beside You,
         and blessed me and dressed me
            for my journey.

You have graced me
   with Your Holy Lovelight—
      may it shimmer and shine
         from deep within me,
            in all my days,
               in all my ways.

I will always sing Your praises.
   And, I will never thirst,
      so long as I am One-with-You—
         so long as You are with me.
         Amen.

CHAPTER EIGHT

PSALM 121

Psalm 121 Let God Help

I gaze upward—
  faraway—
    beyond the hills on the horizon.

I wonder and I marvel
  at how I got to this day,
    to this place,
      to this moment,
        to this state of being,
          to this state of heart,
            to this state of faith.

The ridge of the highest hills
  emerges from behind the clouds.
    And the clouds now whimsically wisp away in the wind.

I now see the sun beyond the ridge,
  rising, radiating, reaching out,
    and greeting me in the morning breeze.

I feel arising in me, a strength, and a power—
  a force that feels somewhat random and nebulous.
    Yet, in the cloud of its mystery and mystique,
      it remains solid, and strong and clear.

It is a life-giving energy,
  a life-giving aura,
    a life-giving Presence.
      You God, are with me.
        Your welcomed and timely help
          grounds me, and stays me.

Here, in the stillness of the morning Light,
　I stand strong, empowered, embraced.
　　I am protected, shielded, safe.
　　　I am ready to face
　　　　the shade, the dark, the night—
　　　　　whatever will come my way, today.

My prayerful heart ascends in song to the hills,
　to the ridge, and beyond.
　　I vow that I will always,
　　　"look to the hills"[1]—Selah

1. paraphrase of NRSV Ps 121: 1

Love

Love—the unfinished masterpiece of the heart—
the poetry, art, and song of its depths—
whose canvas is luminous,
whose form can be lustfully lyrical,
whose harmonies lull, and lift, and linger.
Exquisite and bespoke,
yet, universal and common.

Love—in its simplicity—
is the quintessential glue of life—
the de facto gel of relational passion—
the *'je ne sais quoi bond'* of heart-borne bliss.

Love—in its complexity—
has many vibrant and distinctive faces—
Philia, Pragma, Storge, Eros, Ludus, Mania, Philautia, and Agape!

Wholesome, welcomed and warm.
Cherished, coveted and craved.
Dreamt of, driven by, and dear.

Quivering, shivering,
fervent and free.
Arising from within—
from deep deep deep within,
yet seemingly and somehow,
external, enveloping, embracing—
and all-encompassing.

Rightfully rash or brash.
Rarely random—normally nebulous in the now.

Holding—securely, yet gently.
Holding—yet, freeing.

Swept-off-your-feet, yet, totally grounded and sure.
  Fluid—dynamic, evolving and becoming,
    yet solid and constant—steady and true.

Sweetly sensorial, like the intimacy of full immersion.
  Palpable, like the chest-pounding thrill of decibelic surround sound.
    Enlivened in every breath.

Rendering moments of tenderness, breathlessness,
  completeness, and oneness. Selah

Predictably impetuous in the youth.
  Exhilarating, like the rush and the blush of victory.
    Strong, like sunshine—solar rays at noon in June.
      Feisty-and-protective like a mom for her very young.

Romanced by the sound of the Eternal,
  and the music of the spheres,
    in the river of life,
      in Grand-Canyon-moments,
        in moonlight over waters,
          and in the northern celestial twilight dance
            of the Aurora Borealis.

Mystical and surreal,
  yet tangible and real.

Presents itself as *Wordless Knowing Presence,*
  emerging in a heartwarming Showing—
    a Shimmering, a Glimmering, a Glowing. Selah

Most Integral Fractal of Holy Lovelight—
  given and graced by God.

Always there, for the ready.
   Always there, for the open and receptive.
      Always and ever, love is.
         Always and ever, God is.
         Always and ever, God is love.

Like a canyon, like a crater, like an ocean, like a well—love is

God's Grace

Picture a magnificent waterfall.
  A grand river leaves its lofty headwater highlands,
    and slowly meanders, gradually descending from the heights,
      while traversing both forest and meadow realms.

It quietly carves its course, making its pathway through the lowlands,
  between the unique glacial drumlin hills,
    and the casually rock-strewn-till-plains and fields.

The escarpment looms.
  A giganormous rocky cliff stands up tall, straight and true and sure,
    to greet the fast-flowing waters.

Et Voila!
  The turbulent roiling waters are majestically sent sailing—soaring—
    hurtling airborne high into the heights,
      free to mist and to vaporize,
        and spray and play and cascade,
          falling wherever they will.

The energy is palpable.
  The view is spectacular.
    The sound is thunderous.
      The water itself becomes a gracious gift
        to the stillwater pool of the rivercourse below,
          which humbly lies awaiting—
            in awe and in wonder,
              in eager and hopeful anticipation.

Iridescent intermittent spectral rainbows dance and frolic in the air,
  sparkling and blazing in a free and natural light show,
    hovering and sweetly surrendered
      to the space at the face at the base of the cliff.
        Such an ethereal sight!
        Such a *known* natural wonder,
          yet such a *perceived* fantasy—
          an enchanting mystery full of
          mystique and curiosity!

With this image of the graceful, gleeful, free-falling waterfall
  painstakingly etched into your seeking and contemplative mind,
    now picture the Grace of God,
      pouring out freely, fervently,
        abundantly and perpetually,
        from God to humanity
        and to all of Creation.

Picture that same Grace cresting the ridge of the escarpment of all life,
  and watch it be sent radically and randomly,
    majestically and mystically over the edge,
      into the hearts and into the lives
      of all open and receptive beings.

Grace is a gracious gift of God,
  given freely and abundantly,
    that knows no boundaries, or limits, or time.

God's Grace is so tangibly real
  in the hearts of those who know and love their God.

God's Grace pours out,
  flows in around and through,
    and it reaches into and touches,
      alters, changes, and transforms.

God's Grace is graciously bestowed
on all who open their hearts and their lives to receive.

God's Grace is a mode of transmission,
a veritable vector,
even a mystical wand,
connecting God to the living, breathing world.

God's Grace is a treasure,
of infinite value,
greater than any land-mined gold or jewel,
or priceless pearl of the sea.

Open your heart and your life to the Grace of God,
and come to know and feel
'the power and the magnif and the joy of the gift'.
Let God's Grace grace you.
Let yours be a life-giving Life of Grace.
Always and ever, Amen.

Light Into Dark Into Light Again

Light into dark into Light again.
   Indeed there are Sacred times—
     in birth—in life itself—in death.

Nurses are both honored and privileged,
   to humbly and quietly serve humanity—
     in its Sacredness—
       in these Holy Moments—
         with compassion and understanding—
         pouring the healing Light
        of hope and joy and peace
       into hurting souls—
      or into their
       darkened world.

Nursing care is an expression of God's Love.
   God is the nurse of our body, mind, and spirit.
   Light into dark into Light again. Selah

Where is God?

Where is God, when the expectant parents
  are delivered of a stillborn child?

Where is God, when a traumatized 14 year old rape victim
  takes her own life,
    upon hearing of her rapist's
      lenient sentencing?

Where is God when a drunk driver with a suspended license,
  crashes into and kills an entire young family?

Where is God on the streets
  where the stigma of
    homelessness, addiction and mental illness abounds,
      where the ragged people dwell, in neglect and in insecurity—
        like ghosts and shadows—
          unseen and unfathomed by most?

Where is God, when a seasoned ER team
  is powerless to save their esteemed young colleague
    from catastrophic critical cardiac illness and death?

Where is God, in the war-torn lands,
  where unthinkable crimes, and injustices,
    and savagely cruel indignities have become a way of life?

Where is God??!!

God is in the hearts of all who call upon Him,
  in their time of need.
    God is present
      in all the darkness,
        in all the despair,
          in every discerning heart.

God weeps with.
  God gives hope.
    God's love comforts.
      God's peace heals.
        God leads from darkness into Light.

God calls out to all who sorrow—
  would only our hearts be open
    to His gentleness,
      to His loving-kindness,
        to His Fatherly love.

In the seasons of our life,
  in the Sacredness of our very being,
    with Emmanuel in our hearts—
      God is with us!
        Thanks be to God!

Born of Essential Goodness

A young 'tweenage' girl, in a flash of fiery rage,
   commits a heinous crime,
      targeting the marginal and the fringe.
         Her actions are indeed, socially unjust.
            Her motive is hatred, and it is fuelled by fear.
            Her heart lives in total darkness.

God of all our hearts—
Bless her,
   that she may awaken
      to the essential goodness of her being,
      to the Sacredness of her life—
      to the Sacredness of all life.

Bless her,
   that she may recognize all of her own
      darkness and confusion and falsehoods,
         that she may return to the wholeness,
            to the heart of compassion, respect and love,
            with which she was born.

Bless her and grace her,
   that she may, moving forward, see with the eyes of her heart,
      that she may recover a sense of the Holy Light within,
         that she might in time,
            become the-Light-not-the-darkness
            for all whom she meets.

Hold her, and keep her throughout her days,
   as she struggles,
      as she intentionally transforms
         into her true blessed self, in the Light.
            Bless her intentional life-blessing-return, to the Light.

Bless those in her midst, and those whom she has harmed and hurt,
that they only judge her actions, and not her very being—
that they will look upon her
with hearts of compassion and understanding,
with the humanity and the grace
to love her, to teach her,
to help her, to heal her.
Let them help her to find her Light.

God of Light and love, hear my prayer. Amen.

God of the Threshold
(God of My Liminal Space)

God of the mystery,
  God of the wonder,
    God of the vastness,
      Come to me!

God of the shoreline,
  God of the high place,
    God of the Thin Place,
      Hear my heart!

God of the River,
  God of the Lovelight,
    Ground of All Life and Being,
      Be with me!

God of Living Water,
  Let me not falter,
    My heart's an altar,
      to Your love!

God of my story,
  God in Your glory,
    Present before me,
      I will pray.

God of the weary,
  God of the wary,
    God of the wandering,
      Strengthen me!

God of the joyful,
  God of the gentle,
    God of the journey,
      Grace my heart.

Here as I stumble,
  let me be humble,
    let me not fumble,
      in Your grace.

Here in my yearning,
  here in my discerning,
    here in my turning—
      hear my prayer.

Hear my prayer,
  hear my prayer,
    hear my prayer,
      hear my prayer!

On Michael's Watch

It all seems like a dream—a stupendous Odyssean dream—
  one all-night insatiably erotic and fantasy reverie,
    with a seemingly twisted and incomprehensible storyline!

But, it is real!
The ancient Celtic rites of the Fall Equinox
  at Michaelmas, on St Michael's Day,
    are lush and laden with symbols of hope, fertility, and productivity.

    +++

As if on a great rush of wind, on the gust of a Godly gale, they are off.
  The Oda has begun!
    Wild-eyed men and their young, spirited women
      mount their borrowed and stolen horses, *en masse.*
    No saddles. No bridles. No reins.
    No starting time. No finish line.

Off they are, in a flurry of hooves and mud,
  cavorting playfully in ritualistic riding fervor.
    Eros and energy erupting everywhere!
      The adrenaline rush is wildly contagious.
        And then, in the crisp evening air of late September,
        the public heats of wildness and chaos
        simply and surely transform,
          into the more private lures of libido.

Bidding farewell to their fine equine rides of the day,
   the riders seek out their lovers in the evening shadows,
      in the dusk, in the lust, in the gloaming, and unfolding of the night.
         Lovers-in-love, love-making,
            wild and ripping, bold and gripping—
               an all-evening-and-all-night-frenzy
                  of dance, intimacy and desire—
                     pure and purest pleasures—
                        pure and primal love.

By day, Michael rides his mighty horse
   on a cloud in the great and grand blue dome,
      and watches over the carrot harvest in the fields,
         where the last wild daisies of the Summer season
            breathe and bask and bloom.

He sees lovers gifting their lovers with ribbon-tied carrots,
   in baskets beautifully woven with reeds of hope and promise.
   Not simply phallic,
      carrot giving is a traditional symbolic gift
         of fertility, creativity and productivity.

And by night, Michael safeguards the lovers—
   in the frenzy, and the fury and the fire,
      as they all open their treasures in the twilight.
         His cloud in the darkening sky grows even more fiery,
            in the passion, in the promise—
               in the hope.

+++

A Personal Prayer of Petition for God's Help.

Dear God,
In this fecund and fertile, and widely creative world of Yours,
  my barrenness and my brokenness consume me.

Oh, that I could ever be—so blessed be—with child.
  Oh, that the treasure—the gift of new life within me—
    could soon be ours—could soon be mine.

In earnest, I harvest my carrots,
  with my heart of hope, and humility.
    I honor them, and my husband delights in their promise.

It's not September now, I know,
  and the festival of Michaelmas is long ago passed.
    But please please please, God,
      send Your Holy Angel Michael to me.

Oh God, help me find a wild or stolen horse,
  and let us all ride together,
    in the muck and in the mud,
      in the wildness of wind,
        through the dark, to the Light,
          in your tender blessing,
            unburdened, unbridled and unruly.

Let life and Light quicken in me, this night.
  Grace my life with new life, I pray.
    Amen.

Elephant In My Room

True Friends—
  'Speak' what's on their mind
  'Share' what's on their heart
  'Support' each other—*always.*

When there's an elephant in the room,
  the unspoken, and the unshared are deafening,
    leaving *support* to fly the coup in confusion,
      resulting in complete avoidance,
        and in breakdown of communication.
          And the elephant remains in the room,
            until someone calls it by its name
              and puts it to rest.

True friends know each other's hearts,
  and reach out instinctively
    in joy, in sorrow,
      and in encouragement.

True friends don't hurt each other,
  rather, they take time and take care to—
    Speak what's on their mind—honestly
      Share what's on their heart—openly, and
        Support each other *always—unconditionally.*

193

Dear God,
   There's an elephant in my room,
      and I do not know its name.
         Please help me to escape,
            or give me strength to engage.
         Please, please, please—
            tell me and my friends
               the elephant's name!

Iona, River Me

Iona, river me—to where my heart can see—
  Ferry my faith through space and time,
    to waters sublime, in Presence Divine—
      River me.

Iona, river me—to where my heart can see—
  Deepen my love's compassion,
    in currents of grace, Amazing Grace—
      River me.

Iona, river me—to where my heart can see—
  Swirling in depths of mystery,
    where wisdom and truth, will shore up, renew—
      River me.

Iona, river me—to where my heart can see—
  Pooling my effervescent joy,
    exuberant dance, this Holy romance—
      River me.

Iona, river me—to where my heart can see—
  Cresting the tides of faithfulness,
    with Holy Lovelight, this Ancient Lovelight—
      River me.

Iona > Ee-Shona > Shining Isle > Holy Shining > God.

Vignette—Discernment and Onward

The door closed. It was over.
  A lifetime career of Nursing wound itself down
    much like a blazing bonfire settles down over time
      into fervent radiant embers.
        And with a final flicker and poof of smoke,
          it was gone. Time to move on.
            Move onward.

Time now to discern my new identity. My new pathways.
  Time to allow my creative life-passions to fire up and come alive,
    to lead me onward,
      undaunted, unbridled, on uncharted paths.

Newly retired, I took time to rest, and rest well.
  I lost considerable weight, and went to the pool every day.
    I went on some educational, personal,
      and spiritual retreats, near and far.

I unearthed my amassed collection of books.
  I eagerly dove into reading for my Celtic Wisdom studies.
    I read about the Spiritual Masters,
      and the Christian Mystics.
        And I found a few acclaimed poet's works,
          to study the mastery of their craft.

And, I revisited my own personal trove of unpublished writings,
  in the form of poetry, prayer and prayersongs,
    liturgies, lyrics and full music scores.

I had just literally, closed the door with finality,
  on my employment and on my calling
    in the Compassionate Life,
      and I was virtually flinging the doors wide open
        to both my Contemplative Life
          and my Creative Life.

By intentionally spending a year in transition,
  in personal development, in discernment,
    I'd placed my body mind and spirit
      in a place of readiness, receptivity and openness.

I allowed my floodgates to swing open wide,
  pouring into me, and over me and through me.
    I experienced an uplifting and freeing
      sense of spaciousness and expansiveness,
        and even an earthen-cosmic-grounding-and-
          a-strengthened-bond-of-interconnectedness.

My studies were no longer mere concepts or theories.
  I began to live out and embrace and embody
    their core realities and their simple truths—
      and their pure wisdom.

All the while in my discernment, I received encouragement,
  from friends, family, former colleagues, pastor-friends,
    and from God.
      They were not subtle in their words
        "You need to publish!"

And, "as sure as the sun rose"[1] each and every day,
  God walked with me
    through that whole year of discernment.

I traveled to Iona Scotland on a Celtic Wisdom pilgrimage and retreat.
  I saw firsthand the ancient sites
    of Christian mission and ministry,
      in St Columba Bay and at the Iona Abbey.
        In the Nunnery ruins, I discovered the wonders
          of the strength of the feminine,
            in the early and unfolding Christian story.

1. paraphrase of TNIV Hos 6; 3

On the rugged shores, and at the heights of the hillocks,
   and at the edge of the ancient well at Dun I,
      I stepped into mystical Thin Places—random outdoor locations
         where the separation between human and Divine
            was said to be palpably thin.

In these Thin Places, the power of God
   was so preciously perceptible, and predominant.
   God was present to me.

I was changed. I was open.
   I was transcending into a more spiritual being.
      I was no longer simply well read and educated.
         I stepped through and floated through a grand liminal space
            into the higher ground of experiential faith
               and into the realm of spiritual witness.
                  I was present in Presence.

I can look back with absolute joy and appreciation
   of my previous life and career,
      but as I have now crossed the threshold,
         I stand here with awe,
            breathing in all the mystery and the mystique of the moment,
               filling all my senses
                  with the wonder of the grace of God,
                     and the Presence of God.

I am moving onward. God led me here.
   God nurtured and supported and encouraged me
      on my discernment journey.

My heart is overflowing with gratitude and praise,
   for my God who helped me—
      and who is still helping me find my way.

Thank You God, for Your hand along the way.
   Never did I feel rushed, pushed, pressured or dragged.
    Rather, I was a curling and swirling,
      random and nebulous cloud of Light,
        transforming and transcending slowly,
         through the warmth and the emerging clarity
         of tender dawning Lovelight.

Thank You God
   for being "the mountain from whence cometh my help".[2]
   Thank You God, for keeping me, onward on my journey.

2. NKJV Ps 121:1

Prayer Based on Psalm 121

Dear God,
　Without even a word of my asking,
　　You come.
　　　You help.
　　　　You support and encourage.
　　　　　You set things right in Your own time.

In all my seasons,
　for all my reasons,
　　You God are there for me,
　　　in the highest hills,
　　　　in the morning stillness,
　　　　　in my every breath—
　　　　　　in the altar of my heart.

I lift up my eyes to You—
　I open my heart to You.
　　Together, the road ahead is a straightforward one,
　　　full of hope,
　　　　and the promise of Your help.

Thanks be to You oh God,
　for keeping me
　　for blessing me
　　　for holding me. Amen.

CHAPTER NINE

PSALM 139

Psalm 139 Formed, Known, and Loved by God

How comforting. How affirming.
  How exquisitely rich it is to be known, understood, and sought,
    in every breath,
      in every heartbeat,
        in every step in life's journey.

I sit. I rise. I lay down. I ponder questions and answers. I run and hide.
  And I journey in my heart, mind and soul to places
    near and far, known and unknown, safe and scary.
      I can take wing over the waters,
        and then soar in the heights.
          God knows where I am.

My thoughts, my words, and my doing,
  are all known to God, who knew me before I was born—
    known to God who formed me—
      known to God who calls me beloved.

How grand is this love that holds me,
  that searches me, and knows me through all time?
    Unconditional is not a big enough word!

I am loved by God.
  I transcend in the vastness of His Agape Love.
    I rest, in being known and loved by God.

Gasp of Wonderment

Exquisite.
  Unique.
    Sacred.
      Momentary or lasting.

I gasp in gaping wonderment
  in the witness
    in the experience
      in the aura or realm
        in the beauty
          in the intricate complexity or pure simplicity
        in the wholeness
        in the reality
        in the truth—

in the humbling honor and privilege
  of being part of
    present with
      in the midst of
        blessed by
          and graced by.

And my heart bows, in awe, in gratitude, in reverence.
  For indeed everyone and everything,
    is of the Holy.
      In this very real truth,
        I gasp.
          Hallelujah! Amen!

Soul

Soul—

Cannot be seen.
  Can be heard.
    Can be touched by, moved by, felt deeply—
      sought and lost and found again.

Can connect with
  in ethereal, mysterious, and transcendent ways.

Can energize and incite and ground.
  Similar to, yet much much more than,
    a living inspiration from the depths, or a gut feeling.

Can shape and define and direct one's thinking,
  and one's actions
    and one's life journey.

Soul is truly, an oxymoron of nebulous-clarity-and-depth-of-being!
  It grounds every human being! Selah

Soul is the rich and unique Light
  of the intense interior being.

Soul transcends borders
  of space, time, art, reality, and humanity.

Soul is likened more to gases than liquids,
  in that it moves and disturbs and permeates deeply
    by filtering into and reaching into human depths
      in incomprehensible ways and means.

Soul is a lighthouse, a harbor, a tugboat,
   a birthplace, a center, a hearth,
      a Shepherd, a Pastor, a Guide—
         and passion, and grace, and Light.

My own churning, burning, discerning and affirming soul
   longs, yearns, hopes, and prays.
      The embers of my soul
         light me, lead me, warm me.

By the grace of God,
   God knows my soul.

Soul Friend

Soul Friend—Anam Cara—
   friends connected uniquely and deeply by the Light of Life,
      by their shared experience,
         by a depth of faith inherent in their very being,
            by an intangible knowing and understanding
               of each other's heart.

They hold each other accountable on their faith journeys—
   on their journeys of life.
      They allow wanderings for curiosity and creativity,
         but they admonish when poor paths are chosen,
            and when the way is lost.

They love with honorable love.
   And they hold each other in utmost respect and regard.
      They encourage and support and comfort each other,
         through all the curves of life.

Their Lights broaden together.
   Their rivers-running-deep are a blessed confluence of souls,
      meandering through all time and eternity.

Truly, they know each other's heart,
   as surely as God knows their hearts.

P.S.— I Am Heard, Known and Understood

Thank you from the bottom of my heart, for listening.
  Thank you, for *hearing my heart*.
    Thank you, for your listening presence, when I need it the most.

You give me time and space and freedom,
  to explore my feelings,
    and to express my feelings,
      and even to expand my personal insights and horizons.

Your demeanor is open, accepting, and non-judgmental.
  You welcome my words—
    my random and nebulous and unfinished thoughts,
      my active thinking, and my reactive emotions.

You make me own all of my words and my whims.
  You let my angers boil up, and simmer down,
    without them losing their steam.
      You help me to redirect my angers, my doubts and my fears,
        into pro-active plans and actions.

You channel my energies onto the good path, the right path—
  onto the pathway that serves the greater good.

And, when you respond to me,
  your carefully chosen words not only tell me that you have heard me,
    but that something arose in you, and stirred in you—
      impassioning and empowering you too.

You frame your heart in Holiness—
  pure and fresh and true.
    Your faithfulness runs deep, deep, deep.

Your very presence is sometimes all I need,
　　to shift perspective—
　　　to gain perspective —
　　　　to regain perspective—
　　　　　into the issues and the artworks
　　　　　　that color my soul.

You listen with love and compassion.
　　You listen and *hear with your heart.*
　　　You listen and hear, with the ears of God.

I've been heard. I've been healed.
　　I've been valued. I've been allowed to be real.
　　　I am known and I am impeccably understood.

Thank you just isn't a big enough word,
　　but an Anam Cara doesn't need any thanks or rewards, or prizes.
　　　An Anam Cara, just simply, is.

P.P.S., In my simplest and elementary words,
　　An Anam Cara is
　　　a welcomed-expression-of-God-here-on-earth.
　　　　Thanks be to God for Anam Cara(s).

My Great "I AM"

I am not defined
    by my pain or my sorrow or my fears or my emptiness.
      I am shaped by God's Love.
        And I am known by my love.
          I am healed of all that harms me.

I am strengthened in His ever-presence.
    I serve as a wounded healer.
      I am born with a Servant's Heart.
        I am graced with God's Holy Lovelight
        and this I freely share with those in need.

This is an affirmation of my plain and humble *first person truth*—
    and not the self centered arrogant waxing
      of some self-righteous narcissistic poet.

I am a Child of God.
    I am forgiven.
      I am contented.
        I am loved.
          God loves me with a Father's heart,
            and I love Him.

All is well in my heart and soul.
    Nothing else matters—I am His.
      I am known by God.

And this understanding of the truth brings me—
    peace in my soul,
      joy and hope in my heart,
        and love deep deep deep within.

I am in a very good place—
   my faith journey has brought me here.
     I trust in God. Implicitly.
       I am one-with-God. Explicitly.

Thanks be to God.
   Thanks be to the Shepherd
     who loves me and leads me.
       Thanks be to God
         who knows my heart.

I am blessed.
  I am beloved.
   I am known.
    I am One.
    Amen.

The Best Is Yet To Come

God knows me,
  knows my heart,
    knows my soul,
      knows my all.

And He has promised
  to all who know Him
    and to all who love Him
      and to all who call on Him—

Unique
  Unordered
    Unruly
      Unabashed
        Unbridled
          Unlimited
            Unwavering and
              Ultimately Unconditional
              Love.

And—truly—still—yet—without a doubt—
  the best is yet to come!

Vignette—Known

You know me. You know my heart.
  In my younger and wayward wanderings,
    I filled my life with sports and competition,
      and laughter and carefree living.

I dove deeper, spun higher, ran faster.
  I even ran so fast,
    that my feet were seemingly not even touching the ground!
    And You were there with me God, all along.

I lived in the East, and I journeyed even farther East.
  I trekked to the North and traveled throughout the South,
    and You knew this God,
      and You blessed all of my journeys.
        Someday, I will head West!

I yearned and dreamed big,
  so very big,
    and I almost lost my way.
      I lost sight of goodness, wholeness, and oneness.
        My *separateness* was unruly, unholy,
          and it was insidiously hurting me.

And then, I was struck down hard.
  A life-changing injury
    and a life-altering illness
      all but stopped me in my tracks.
        No more training or competition for me.
          Never, ever again.

At first I was angry, spiteful and tormented with my losses.
But as time passed,
I realized that the unwelcomed hindrances
of injury and illness were not disgraces,
rather, they were gifts of grace from You, God,
were I only spiritually mature enough
to recognize this at the time.

For my injury and illness caused me to draw so close to You.
They led me into the actively contemplative realm.

Opening before me was a much slower pace and a deeper world—
a lifetime of musing
on all things that mattered most—
A spiritual journey
defined more by my questions
than by my answers—
A creative and expressive world
in lyrics and liturgy,
in poetry and prose,
and in melody, music
and metaphor.

I am grateful for the life I've been given.
I delight that in my phenomenal faith journey,
I have come to understand—
and experience—
the wonders of the words
Beloved, His, Chosen, and *Called*.

I am Yours God.
  I delight in being known by You,
    formed by You,
      sought by You,
        found by You,
          and loved by You.

I pray that You will
  always know me, God,
    always lead me,
      always hold me safe,
        in life, in death,
          in body mind and spirit,
            in my traipsing and in my transcendence,
            in my here and now,
              in my always,
                and in my evermore.
                Amen.

Prayer Based on Psalm 139

Dear God,
  You know my heart.
    You know my soul.
      And I delight in being sought by You,
        as I wander and dance through life.
          I delight in being found by You,
            and welcomed home.

I am nourished and nurtured,
  fueled and fed,
    simply in the knowing of Your want for me.

You search me.
  You reach out.
    You call to me.
      You hold me in Your love.

I am blessed.
  I am grateful.
    I am humbled.

Thanks be to You, oh God,
  for forming me,
    finding me,
      feeding me,
        and filling me. Amen.

CHAPTER TEN

PSALM 150

Psalm 150 Celebrate God!

Arise! Come alive!
  Be festive! Sparkle and fizz—and light up the town! Effervesce!
    Dance freely in your own emanant iridescence!
      Celebrate the wonder and the power
        and the grace and the love
        and the Holy ever-presence
          of our gracious and giving God.
            All honor, praise and glory
              be to God!

Let us *all* sing! *Out loud!!!*
  Shout and sing! *Loud, loud, louder!!!*
    Parade and prance with excitement!
      Worship with fervor and exuberance and great joy!
        Our God is Holy, Sacred, Divine.
          Our God is awesome, magnificent,
            and alive in our hearts.

How can we keep from singing out our joy, in worship, song and prayer?
  Let no one ever silence the praise on our lips
    or the joy in our hearts
      or the faith in our Living Loving God.

Let the mountaintops sing and the wide valleys ring
  in echoes of praise, in anthems ablaze, alive in the grandeur of faith.

Celebrate with great noise and conviction, our great and glorious God!

Hallelujah!

Hallelujah—
  An utterance given to God—
    in praise,
      in gratitude,
        in affirmation.

Deeply heartfelt.
  Arising from the depths of faith—
    intuitively, reverently, spontaneously.

Leonard-Cohen-style passionate chorus,
  versus singular whispered word,
    versus grand cathedral antiphonal choral responses.

Stirring, moving, touching.
  Bringing God into the moment—
    so very tangibly into the present moment.

Calming, calling, celebratory.
  Centering, connecting, completing.
    Stepping into wholeness, Presence, Oneness.
      Roisterous, unruly, and raucous,
        or, breathy, beholding and beseeching.

Call out to God "*Hallelujah*"—in the Light, in the dark, in the now,
  in the chaos, in the calm—in all the complex continuing curves of life.
    Let the Hallelujah grace your lips—enlivening your very soul.

And I lift my voice to shout out with joy
"I am born of God—
born of the Light—
the Holy Lovelight of God—
God is with me—
Hallelujah!
Hallelujah!!
Hallelujah!!!
Amen".

The Fire In My Heart

The fire dwindles, embers glowing, warmth radiating.
  Not a breeze to flicker, or to flame up.
    All is peaceful, calm, settled.

Along comes a breath, a wind, a flow of air passing by.
  Ashes swirl. A smoldering cloud arises.
    Tiny sparks rise up and shoot across,
      into a nebulous cloud of wispy grey smoke.

An ember ignites—
  flaring up, flashing fine tongues of fire,
    licking outward into the space.
      And, another.

The fire is active again.
  Excited.
    At first, tentative.
      Receiving more support now
        from a continuous breeze.

The fire rants and rages—
  with passion but not in anger!
    Fueled by the unseen.
      Arising smoke billows upwards—
        heat emanating,
          sparks flying in frenzied flight.

And again, the fire's fury dissipates,
  and the flaming sparkly silhouette shrinks once more,
    retreating into its sweet glowing embers,
      in readiness—
        in mindful presence—
          in stillness.

The fire is my love—
My love for God.
Born of the Light of God within me.
It never goes out. It never dies.
As with God, there is no darkness, only Light.
In my heart,
there is always my fire, always my love.

A love that ignites the passion of my faith,
and "stirs into flame, all of my God-given gifts."[1]
And, in this Light, with my fiery love and gratitude,
my fire bursts
into emblazoned celebrations of worship,
in song, and dance, and prayer.

This ritual fire-dance of my love
kindles my faith,
nurtures my heart,
stirs my soul.

This infernal core of mine is eternal.
My love for God is eternal, as is His Love for me.
I shall rise up and celebrate, and shout Hallelujah!

"And, as sure as the sun rises"[2],
as I worship God,
my love, my fire,
is sparkling, crackling and blazing!

And so I shout out in song
"Hallelujah! Amen!"

1. paraphrase of NRSV 2 Timothy 1: 6
2. TNIV Hos 6: 3

Come To The Altar

Come. Walk. Run.
   Allow yourself to be carried.
      Pause before the altar of your choosing.
         Stop all movement and thinking, and just be.
            Give permission if you need to,
               for time to move along as it will.

Simply empty yourself of all your worries, your angst, your cares.
   Confess your falsehoods,
      your shortcomings and your wanderlusting wavering path.
      Be still.
         Still, be still.
            Still still still—be still.

As you enter deeply into the silence,
   release your overwhelming needs for power, control,
      authority, and independence.
         Humble yourself.
            And, as you do,
               feel an ethereal lightness
               wash over your soul.

And, when you have lightened up,
   you will sense a refreshing openness,
      a readiness, a healing, or a wholeness—
         an all encompassing Lovelit aura of peace
         will settle in, around, and through you.

You're not done yet!
   Cherish this peace.
      Savor this peace.
         Dwell in this peace.
            For it is a gift from God.

A freely given gift from God of your heart.
Stop again, all your energies, and just listen,
attuning only to the wonders of the Sacred,
in this moment, and in this place.

God is with you! Know it! Feel it!
Let God's love stir deeply in your soul,
that you will aspire to find ways to share this love—always.

At the right time, lift your eyes upward.
The Holy, The Sacred, The Divine—
unseen but so very real—is with you!

Arise!
Ephphatha!
Be open!
Sing!
Dance!
Shout out praises to God!

God is with you always—
at the altar, in the altars of the world, in the altar of your heart,
in your mindfulness, in your heartfulness,
in your waking and sleeping, and in your coming and going—
always, always, always.

All praise be to God
who graces us all with His Presence!
God is present in your presence—
Praise! Praise! Praise!

Come to the altar now.

 Come intentionally into God's Presence.

  Come, in the assurance, in the comfort, and in the strength
of God's unconditional love.

   Sense it!

    Savor it!

     Celebrate it!

    Amen!

My God-With-Me-Life

Emmanuel—1st century vocabulary.
  God-with-me—21st century vocabulary.
    Not just church words,
      rather, my very own emotional and spiritual reality—
        my very own moment-by-moment, breath-by-breath,
          in-every-spec-and-space-and-spin-experience
            of God's Presence.

I seem to go on and on and on about the poetic Holy Lovelight,
  and I make no apologies for this.
    In my exquisite and breathtaking faith journey,
      my experience of God-with-me,
        is truly a luminous-living-breathing-Light-experience.
        It is a totally tangible ethereal luminescence,
          that is unequivocally grounding, earthy,
            and deeply connecting.

I have been held in the Light, filled by the Light,
  warmed by the Light, led by the Light,
    harbored in the Light—
      and loved in the Light.

God is known to me, and shown to me—in the Light.
  I am known to God—in the Light.
    And yes, "as sure as the sun rises"[1] each day,
      God *is* with me—in the Light.

And this *is not* simply, a dramatic and eloquent affirmation.
  This *is* my painstaking detailing
    of the most profound and intimate
      Divine-Human-experience,
        and Divine-Human-relationship that can exist!

1. TNIV Hos 6:3

And this, is mine.
　All mine, but not mine alone.
　　My God-with-me is an Omni-God—
　　　for me, and for you,
　　　　and for all who open their hearts to a life with God.

In my heartwarming, faith-warming, life-giving, God-With-Me-Life,
　I dance.
　　I sing.
　　　I step out and I step up.
　　　　I shout for joy.

And with gratitude, I celebrate and I praise God
　for the Sacredness,
　　for the blessedness,
　　　and for all of the wonders and the deets
　　　　of my God-With-Me-Life.

Mine, is a wholesome and fulfilling God-With-Me-Life.
　I am centered. I am whole. I am One.
　　Thanks be to God—God-with-me!
　　　Amen.

Beloved In the Bleak Malevolence

Human appetites for power, authority and control are ravenous.
  In the angry, mean-spirited, and sadly loveless world, I am—
    held at arms length, held at bay, held back,
      shamed, shunned, silenced,
        undervalued, underrated, underestimated,
          misunderstood, misinterpreted, misrepresented.

I am also
  judged-misjudged-and-feared,
    labeled, lorded over, left alone-abandoned,
      controlled, held in contempt, conspired against,
        demeaned, disrespected, despised.

But, in this malicious, unmerciful, maelstrom of worldly ways
  never, ever, is any of this, by God.
    In the healing waters of the Siloam pool,
      in the tranquil infinity pool of God's loving world,
        in my 24/7 God-With-Me-Life,
          God calls me *Beloved.*

God embraces me and delights in me—
  in all that is me.
    God opens the eyes of my heart.
      My heart sees!!!
        I bask in these words,
          and I stand tall in His call—
            My heart soars and sings!!!

God wants me and needs me, and I want and need God.
  God is present to me, no matter what.
    God brings Light into my worldly-darkened-world.

God graces me with the Holy Lovelight.
  From the midnight mayhem of malevolence,
    amid all of the mad and mighty masks of malevolence,
      and in the brazen blur of bleak malevolence,
        I emerge, healed, strengthened and empowered,
          full of grace, in the Light.
            I arise,
              with eyes wide open,
                and with heart wide open,
                  as *God's Beloved.*

With my heart of gratitude and praise,
  I inwardly say
    "Thanks be to God—my heart smiles!"
      With euphoria bubbling up from deep inside of me,
        my heart leaps and laughs
          as I call out loudly *"Feel my joy God—See my joy!"*

From the very depths of my humble beloved-ness
  I celebrate with my own words
    of sheer exuberance and praise
      "God is with me—Hallelujah—Amen!"

Vignette—Gratitude and Praise

It's all about gratitude and praise.
  Come shout and sing with my heart!!

Long story made short.
  The pain was awful. Almost unbearable.
    But, I had to go on.
      I had to move forward on my journey.
      I could not stop-in-my-tracks now.

I was on a mission to find and experience a Thin Place.
  I needed to find a Thin Place.
    I was so open to an encounter with The Holy,
      that it drove me to 'move through' the pain.
        I had come all this way.
        I was in pain, so much pain,
          yet I was so open, so ready, so primed.

I got on the ferry, miserable, almost in tears.
  This was the last leg of the journey,
    and I would then be there.
      With a damp and misty and grey sky hovering close,
        we traversed the Sound in a filmy fog,
          and we disembarked on the Holy Isle.

Before I could even tune into the unique Sacredness,
  the inherent Holiness,
    or even the calm of the coveted shores,
      I tuned in once more to my pain.

It was GONE!!! Simply GONE!!!
  I was free! I was freed!
    It is not clear to me, exactly *when* I was healed—
      during boarding or boating,
        or upon setting foot on the shore,
          but I first noticed my 'painfree-ness'
            as I walked away from the boat.

God came to me, and met me in my need.
  God healed me.
    And God blessed me
      as I began my new faith journey—
        on a pilgrimage of a lifetime.

My smile broadened.
  Tears of joy flowed.
    Gratitude filled my heart
      and washed over me
        like the rolling swells of the ocean waves
          in the Sound.

This vignette *is not* about pain.
  Nor about healing.
    Nor about God's Presence and Providence.

It is about gratitude and praise.
  A state of heart overflowing with currents and eddies,
    and stationary-erupting-standing-waves,
      which are alive with fervent and joyful praises to God.

My own heart was bursting with gratitude and praise for God.
My own songs welled up.
There were no angelic choirs,
or heavenly hosts playing archaic stringed instruments.
No trumpets sounding.
No horns echoing
in the heights or on the hillocks.

Nothing but the sounds of
my own thunderous tsunami
of songful praise in my soul,
and the giganormous crashing,
and cascading waterfall of my joy.
Joy of my standing—
and joy of my being—
in a Thin Place—there—
in the very Presence of God.

There *are* Thin Places in our world—there *are* places of this world—
where the finest, thinnest veil
is lifted aloft and fearlessly flung far far away,
off the heights and the windswept shores—
revealing the Holiness, the Sacredness, the One Divine—
revealing the veritable nearness
shared by humans and the Divine—
revealing the precious palpable Presence—
might we only attune ourselves
to this pure and simple truth.

And I am ecstatic and ever-grateful to know this firsthand.

All praise and honor and celebration of my God—
 God of my heart—
  God of my faith journey—
   God of all Thin Places, near and afar!
    I will shout and sing Hallelujah!
    Thanks be to God!
    Thanks be to God—
     right here, right now!
     Amen and Amen!!

Prayer Based on Psalm 150

Dear God,
  I celebrate You.
    I worship You and honor You.

Whether in the stillness of my being,
  or in the majestic fanfare
    of a grand massed choir with philharmonic orchestra,
      or, in my quiet prayerful utterances throughout my day,
      You God are the centre of my life,
        the centre of my faith,
          the centre of my being.

My heart explodes like fireworks, in gratitude for You.
  In my very depths, the Holy Light within me
    is a frenzied fiery laser light show—
      a sparkling iridescent showing
        of the Holy Lovelight
          arises from within me.

With every blessed breath, I praise You.
  In all my fervently emanating sparkle and glow, I praise You.
    Let all that has breath[1]—let all that stirs with Light and life—
      let all form that is born of God—
        honor You, worship You, and celebrate You,
          for always and forever. Amen.

1. NRSV Ps 150: 6

Last Word—
10-Psalm Prayerful Benediction

It's time now to collect all of my random and nebulous thoughts,
   in a prayerful benediction
      of enlightenment and illumination—and hope.

In a world of pathways,
   and new directions, and choices along the way,
      it is good to know that God goes with you.
         It is good for you to choose to turn to God,
            in the face of these decisions and directions,
               and sometimes undeniably difficult choices.

God, like a Shepherd with his flock,
   will search for you,
      will find you,
         and will lead you on in the Light.
         Always.

Like an ancient well of wisdom,
   God has a profound depth that calls out to your depths,
      beckoning you into a stirring Contemplative Life,
         full of Shimmerings, and Shinings,
            Presence and Holy Lovelight.
               Answer the call
                  and *go deep*
                    in your Contemplative Life!

As you draw into stillness, in solitude, present in the moment,
   you will experience a grand spaciousness and expansiveness,
      of body mind and spirit,
         and you will *know and see, Light and clarity,*
            as you have never known and seen before.
            "Be still and know."[1]

1. NRSV Ps 46:10

You were born of God, of 'original blessing', *not* of 'original sin'.
Live strong, and sparkle vibrantly, in this faith-altering-Celtic-truth!
Stand tall as you emerge from the darkness and the oppression
of a sin-based credence and faith tradition.
Yet, still take the time to humble yourself before God,
being honest, ever-accountable and true,
and empty your heart
of all falseness and falsehoods.
God forgives and starts again fresh,
out of an exquisite and tenacious love
for all of His beloved children.
There is such comfort in living
in God's forgiveness and compassion—
a warm and intimate sensation
of being held and made whole, always.

Walk on, strong, sure, safe, with God in your heart.
You will always be more, with God.

God's very Presence and God's very real provision
are gifts freely given to all those
who are open and receptive to God.

When you least expect it, God's help will come to you,
both in the obvious and in the barely perceptible ways.
Cherish the ever-flowing, ever-billowing,
ever-abundant grace of God.

Delight in knowing—
that you were—that you are—
formed by God,
known by God,
and sought by God, always.
For God knows your heart,
and delights in you!

Open yourself—
  radically and joyfully
    in body mind and spirit—
      to your God!
        Honor, worship and celebrate
          God of your heart,
            God of Creation,
              God of Holy Lovelight.
                See the Sacredness inherent in all of life,
                  and sing out songs of praise and gratitude
                    for all the wonders, and wildness,
                      and wisdom of God.

Go now in your blessed One-With-God Life.
  In the beauty and wonder of your
    random and nebulous Lovelit life—
      in the Sacredness of your very being—
        center yourself with God.
          God is with you. Always. Amen. Selah

The Lord's Prayer of the New Millennium—May It Be So

God of all life and being,
   Your Name is Sacred.
      You are Holy. Beloved. Cherished.
         Your Presence nurtures us—here and now.
            Your Way is our way—may it always be so.

Through each and every day, let no being live in hunger or in thirst,
   as You feed and strengthen their souls with Your love.

Please grace our hearts with Your forgiveness—
   and then open up our hearts, to forgive.

Please guide us on our journey, in our discernment of right and wrong.
   And help us to step out of our own darkness,
      that we may come along, to live in Your Light.

For You are The Light of Life—
   The Light of the World—
      The Holy Lovelight in all our hearts.

In gratitude, in reverence,
   in mystery, in delight, in wonder and in awe—Amen.

This prayer, this plea, this intention—
   May it be so. May it be so—for always and forever. Amen.

My Very Own Desiderata 2020

Breathe. Breathe deeply and freely. Just breathe, knowing and trusting
that you are here, that you are home,
and, that this wide wide world is your very own place in the universe.
You are welcome here. It is good and right for you to be here.

Seek to know your world,
and choose to be a unique and vibrant part of it!
Live in all of the truths that have been revealed thus far,
and help to uncover new and more sustainable truths.
Let wisdom befriend you and be your guide.

Stand justly.
Breathe kindness.
And walk humbly with the God of your heart.[1]
Deep calls out to Deep.[2]
Delight in—and dwell in—Holy Mystery!

Respect your world, and all life living therein.
See and honor the Sacred in all of Creation—always.
Do to and for others, as you would have them do to and for you[3].
This golden rule is universally sound,
and is wholesomely grounding—
it is an awesome and an all-round way of living.

Know love, in your heart,
and be love, in your world.
Share your love in all you say and do and think.
Journey on, as you live the Compassionate Life,
and care more for the needs of others
than you do for your own.

1. paraphrase of NRSV Micah 6: 8
2. paraphrase of NRSV Ps 42: 7
3. paraphrase of NRSV Matt 7: 12

And don't forget to love yourself,
  just as you inclusively love all of your neighbors,
    and strangers, and others—alike.

Let your compassion flow,
  just like the soft and warming Light
    that emanates from deep deep deep within your soul.
      Be the Light for those in the dark.

Come to know and understand, and cherish the Holy Lovelight.
  Make the Lovelight come alive in your life—
    in your own colorful images,
      in your own carefully chosen words,
        in the powerful poetry of your own tender faith.
          Let Lovelight be your guiding light—
            your one-bright-star—
              your very own true north.

Be a river,
  one that meanders and flows and surges onward
    in the watercourse of life,
      confidently and surely
        around the bends and the blind curves,
          intrepidly through the treacherous rapids,
            and exuberantly over the cliffs and escarpments,
              just like a magnificent waterfall.

Just be. Just go. Just move forward—
  with hope, with energy and joy, in all your living days.

In this ever-changing world that we all live in together,
  choose to live by this personal mantra—
    or feel free to compose a mantra
      in your own impassioned words!—
        Be the River. Be the Light. Be the Love.

Go now in grace, and serve humanity.
　Go now with a greater sense of spaciousness and expansiveness
　　in body, mind and spirit.

Enter into all of life's grand forests and garden groves—
　in wonderment and in awe,
　　and smell the richness of the evergreens,
　　　and the fragrance of all of the sweet and spicy magnolia blossoms
　　　on your path.

And on every step along the way, breathe deep.
　Just—breathe.

While there in the garden,
　look for and savor the Sacred—
　　linger in the Lovelight—
　　　it is in, within, around and arising from—
　　　all that lives and breathes.

In the stillness and in the freshness,
　be still—just breathe.
　　Amen.